AMERICANS IN BLACK AFRICA UP TO 1865

HOOVER INSTITUTION STUDIES: 5

AMERICANS IN BLACK AFRICA UP TO 1865

By
CLARENCE C. CLENDENEN
and
PETER DUIGNAN

The Hoover Institution
on War, Revolution, and Peace

Stanford University
1964

The Hoover Institution on War, Revolution, and Peace, founded at Stanford University in 1919 by Herbert Hoover, is a center for advanced study and research on public and international affairs in the twentieth century. The views expressed in its publications are entirely those of the authors and do not necessarily reflect the views of the Hoover Institution.

© 1964 by the Board of Trustees of
the Leland Stanford Junior University

All rights reserved

Library of Congress Catalog Card Number: 64-8679
Printed in the United States of America

382.09
C627a

PREFACE

This monograph is second in a series which began with The United States and the African Slave Trade, 1619-1862 (Hoover Institution, 1963, 72 pp.) and is part of a larger general investigation on United States involvement in Africa. (The monograph following this will treat the period from 1865 to 1900.) Criticism and information are welcomed in order to improve these short essays before the whole study appears as a book.

Our purpose has been to set down a general outline of United States activity in Africa. We have concentrated on the American aspect of African affairs and have said little about African reactions to American merchants, missionaries, and explorers. The study is based primarily on printed sources (except for several doctoral dissertations and the private papers of three men) and represents a synthesis of historical scholarship. Much of the information, however, was mined from American memoirs and autobiographies, missionary reports, and government dispatches and these sources have been almost entirely ignored by European, American, and African scholars. It is our hope that others will be encouraged to work on the subject and unearth further facts. Given the lack of previous research on America's role in Africa (two notable exceptions being the work of Norman Bennett of Boston University and George Shepperson of Edinburgh University), we have had to concentrate on narrative rather than on interpretation or analysis.

Many friends and colleagues read and criticized the manuscript: Professor Thomas Bailey of Stanford University, Dr. Lewis Gann of the Hoover Institution, Dr. George Brooks of Indiana University, Dr. Norman Bennett of Boston University, Dr. John Peterson of Kalamazoo University, Dr. J.G. St Clair Drake of Roosevelt University, Professor Peter Bauer of the London School of Economics, and Professor George Shepperson of Edinburgh University.

The authors take full responsibility for any errors that remain, and the opinions and judgments expressed here are theirs alone.

Clarence C. Clendenen

Peter Duignan

20947

CONTENTS

I. AMERICAN TRADERS

The slave trade dominated the relations of Europe and America with Africa until well into the nineteenth century, but Americans and Europeans went to Africa for other reasons as well, both commercial and altruistic.

It has become conventional to draw a distinction between the slave trade and "legitimate" commerce, but until the legal abolition of the slave trade by the United States Congress in 1808, this was as legitimate a form of commercial enterprise as any other. Except for the Quakers and some other humanitarians, few people objected to the traffic in human beings. Hence, it is difficult to draw a fine line between "legitimate" trade and the more spectacular traffic in "black ivory." Probably most of the ships that sailed to Africa from Europe or America in the seventeenth and eighteenth centuries went for slaves, but there was an understanding that the shipmasters were to earn a profit for the owners by any means possible. The few available records indicate that ships bound for the African coasts usually carried a considerable bulk of general trade goods, as well as the rum, brandy, and tobacco that were the recognized mediums of exchange for slaves, and that ships returning to America or Europe from Africa generally carried varying amounts of African products other than human chattel.[1]

American trade developed simultaneously on both African coasts,

---

[1] This monograph will not discuss the participation of the United States in the slave trade. For accounts of American involvement in the slave trade see Warren S. Howard, _American Slavers and the Federal Law, 1837-1862_ (Berkeley, Calif., 1963); Daniel P. Mannix, _Black Cargoes: A History of the Atlantic Slave Trade, 1518-1865_ (New York, 1962); Peter Duignan and Clarence Clendenen, _The United States and the African Slave Trade, 1619-1862_ (Stanford, Calif., 1963).

largely through the efforts of a relatively small group of merchants in a single New England commercial community; American trade with Africa was a near monopoly of Salem. Nevertheless, in many particulars, the commerce of one coast differed from the commerce of the other, and the geographical areas involved are so vast that, for clarity in discussion, it is convenient to draw a purely arbitrary distinction between commerce with West Africa and commerce with eastern and southern Africa.

West Africa

Direct commercial relations between America and Africa seem to have developed first on the West Coast, where the close union between the slave trade and legitimate commerce in the colonial era is illustrated by a venture undertaken by the Beekmans, a prominent merchant family of New York, in 1748. Late in that year they dispatched their brig Revenge to the Gambia, on a speculative voyage, and loaded it with the usual quantities of rum, along with "musketts," brass pans and basins, and other odds and ends. Months later, when the owners had almost given up the Revenge as lost, she sailed into New York Bay, badly battered, but still afloat, and carrying, in addition to forty-five slaves, seventy-nine ounces of gold dust and three and a half tons of dyewood. She had arrived at the African coast at a time when the market was glutted. Consequently, most of her cargo was untouched, but the slaves, the gold dust, and the dyewood together prevented the Beekmans from suffering a ruinous loss.[2]

Probably the first American vessels to arrive in African waters without any interest in slaves were the whaling ships. Whalers are known to have reached the Guinea coast as early as 1763, and Edmund Burke, in his famous speech on "Conciliation with the Colonies" in 1775,

---

[2] Philip L. White, The Beekmans of New York in Politics and Commerce, 1647-1877 (New York, 1956), pp. 309-311, 329-330.

declaimed, "We know that...some of them draw the line and strike the harpoon on the coast of Africa."[3]

Although whalers were not engaged in commerce in the usual sense of that term, there can be little doubt that they purchased provisions, refilled their water butts, and bought small amounts of native wares when they touched land.

American legitimate trade with Africa came into existence after the Revolutionary War. The period following the war was an era in which the American merchants and shipowners, freed from the restrictions of British mercantilism, were feeling their way over the world, searching for markets, hunting for cargoes and salable commodities. In the summer of 1783 Moses Brown, a wealthy Quaker merchant and shipowner of Providence, Rhode Island, and (unlike some of his family) an uncompromising enemy of the slave trade, heard rumors that the prominent firm of Clark and Nightingale was fitting a ship for a slaving voyage to the Guinea coast. Brown protested vigorously, and was informed that the objective of the voyage was not slaves, but "ivory, wax and gold dust." Although there is some indication that Clark and Nightingale were actually covering up their real purposes, the incident is significant as showing that commodities other than slaves attracted the attention of American merchants.[4]

---

[3]See Paul Elmo Hohman, The American Whaleman: A Study of Life and Labor in the Whaling Industry (New York, 1928), p. 28. The Browns of Providence, R.I., between 1769 and 1774 sent whaling vessels regularly to the African coast. James B. Hedges, The Browns of Providence Plantations: Colonial Years (Cambridge, Mass., 1952), pp. 87-88.

[4]Mack Thompson, Moses Brown, Reluctant Reformer (Chapel Hill, N.C., 1962), p. 175. Unfortunately there are very few sources or dependable secondary studies covering American commercial activities in West Africa before 1865. An exception to this general statement, and an authority upon which the present authors have drawn heavily, is George E. Brooks, "American Legitimate Trade with West Africa,

The establishment of the British colony for free Negroes at Sierra Leone in 1787 marked the beginning of a significant change in the economy of West Africa. Sierra Leone became not only a colony for freed slaves and after 1807 a base for the Royal Navy's operations against the slave trade, but also a center of legitimate trade. American trade goods, such as rum and tobacco, once used almost exclusively for the purchase of human beings, became items of exchange for palm oil, dyewoods, and, after 1830, the peanut.

American commercial opportunities on the African coast were stimulated sharply by the long series of wars that started with the French Revolution and lasted until 1815. With shipping from France and other Continental countries driven from the seas, with British shipping pre-empted by the government or harassed by French privateers, the European stations and factories on the African coast became virtually dependent upon American merchants and shipping for both necessities and luxuries. European traders were unable to do business with African customers unless they could offer trade goods, which they could purchase only from the Yankees. Americans were able to obtain cloth from

---

1789-1914" (unpublished Ph.D. dissertation, Boston University, 1962); hereafter cited as Brooks. See also John Carroll Brent, "Leaves from an African Journal," Knickerbocker Magazine, XXXIII (1849), 41-48, 116-127, 206-215, 334-340, 399-409; XXXIV (1850), 127-133, 227-234, 300-305; T. Edward Bowdich, Excursions in Madeira and Porto Santo, during the Autumn of 1823, while on His Third Voyage to Africa (London, 1825); Jacinto Pereira Carneiro, "Memoir on the Trade to the West Coast of Africa Northward of the Equator," Nautical Magazine and Naval Chronicle for 1855, pp. 407-415; Joshua A. Carnes, Journal of a Voyage from Boston to the West Coast of Africa, with a Full Description of the Manner of Trading with the Natives on the Coast (Boston, 1852); Joseph Hawkins, A History of a Voyage to the Coast of Africa and Travels into the Interior of That Country (Philadelphia, 1797); Reverend Charles W. Thomas, Adventures and Observations on the West Coast of Africa and Its Islands (New York, 1860); Commander Thomas Miller, "Western Africa: Its Coast, Resources, and Trade," Nautical Magazine and Naval Chronicle for 1855, pp. 291-296, 345-355.

India and the products of the East Indies, as well as commodities from North America. In 1809, Governor Thompson, of Sierra Leone, reported regretfully to Lord Castlereagh: "I have the honour to represent to your Lordship that this Colony has hitherto been in a great measure supplied with the articles of trade with the Natives by the Americans, particularly with cotton cloths." A year later he morosely reported again: "The cargoes of the Americans consisted in a great measure of India Cloths of the kind principally used in bartering with the Natives." Because of unfavorable financial regulations, he added, the Americans could supply these goods at a much lower price than the British merchant had to pay the East India Company to purchase them.[5]

This condition continued in spite of interruptions caused by President Jefferson's embargo (1807-1809) and the Royal Navy's flagrant disregard of neutral rights on the African coast as well as in European and North American waters.[6] Between 1793 and 1812, American rum, beef, flour, tobacco, and lumber became necessities in West Africa, especially in Sierra Leone. The colony was almost isolated from Europe, and colonists and officials found themselves unable to subsist upon local products--especially with no European trade goods to exchange. Except for American ships and traders, Europeans in Africa would have been in acute discomfort, if not actual hardship. This condition was accentuated in Sierra Leone by the fact that a large part of the colonists were Americans, or the offspring of Americans,

---

[5] Quoted in Brooks, pp. 56-57.

[6] See Robert Greenhalgh Albion and Jennie Barnes Pope, Sea Lanes in Wartime: The American Experience, 1775-1942 (London, 1943), pp. 99-102; Anna Cornelia Clauder, American Commerce as Affected by the Wars of the French Revolution and Napoleon, 1793-1812 (Philadelphia, 1932), passim.

who had a distinct taste for things American.[7] The War of 1812, however, interrupted American activities on the African coast and brought considerable discomfort to the scanty European population, then cut off from practically all sources of supply.[8]

With the restoration of peace in 1815, American ships and traders returned to Africa at once, but conditions had changed. After years of war, the merchants and shipowners of London, Liverpool, and Paris were hungry for business and profits and were not disposed to look kindly upon the interlopers from across the Atlantic. The government officials of Great Britain and France felt the same; in the capitals the old mercantilistic theories had not lost their vitality, and the governing classes believed that they must, by any and all means, promote the trade of their own countries and exclude competitors. Immediately after the close of the wars, by various expedients ranging from preferential duties to outright prohibition of trade with foreigners, the British and French governments attempted to close their African bases to Americans. Within a short time only the small Dutch and Danish factories remained officially open to international trade.

---

[7] A very large number--possibly a majority--of the original colonists in Sierra Leone were American Negroes who had escaped from their masters and fought on the British side in the Revolutionary War. After the war the British took them to Nova Scotia, where they were completely destitute. It was decided to transport them to Africa. See E.G. Ingham, Sierra Leone after a Hundred Years (London, 1894), pp. 8-10, and Christopher Fyfe, A History of Sierra Leone (London, 1962), pp. 31-35.

[8] For an exhaustive discussion of the fact that not all American ships on the African coast were slavers see Brooks, chap. ii. Legitimate American trade is illustrated by one of the first captures made by the British in the war--that of the brig Federal, commanded by Captain Samuel Swan, Jr., bound from Africa to Boston, and laden with "ivory, coffee, palm oil, old copper." Albion and Pope, Sea Lanes in War Time, p. 114. Swan had made several voyages to Africa, all of them in legitimate trade.

Attempts to keep out American (and other) competition were foredoomed to failure. Many traders in Africa, whether European or native, were unimpressed by restrictionist arguments; they saw no reason for confining their trade to Europeans when Americans supplied what they wanted at a substantially lower price than was demanded in England or France and would give a higher price for whatever the trader had to sell. And the Americans had no qualms about smuggling when necessary. Consequently, even in the face of duties intended to be prohibitive and despite the efforts of conscientious officials, American trade with West Africa flourished. In 1822, for example, the British merchants of Sierra Leone, in a petition to Governor MacCarthy by which they hoped to check the alarming increase in American trade, stated that while the British trade with the Gold Coast was £118, 636, American trade had reached £40, 000.[9]

It would be profitless to go into the details of the rather slow and uneven abandonment by the European powers of restrictionist theories and practices in Africa. The change was, of course, closely linked with the rise of free trade theories in Europe, and particularly in Great Britain; nevertheless, the uninhibited Yankee shipmaster and trader had something to do with convincing the authorities of the utter futility of trying to enforce restrictions and maintain national monopolies.

In Sierra Leone and on the Gold Coast, efforts to eliminate Americans and make the areas a complete British commercial monopoly stemmed largely from the efforts of a single official, Governor Charles MacCarthy. He was a soldier by profession. In 1814 Governor Maxwell, of Sierra Leone, returned to England. MacCarthy, who was in command of the British garrison in Senegal, became acting governor, and a year later was confirmed as permanent governor of the colony. Able, conscientious, and conservative, he was guided by an almost

---

[9]Brooks, p. 159.

fanatical devotion to the British monarchy. He had served in the British army in Canada, and to his dislike of American republicanism seems to have been added a thorough distrust of American expansionist proclivities. When such a man received a royal command to enforce the Navigation Laws and exclude American shipping, his orders would be enforced rigidly and without deviation. Consequently, American ships were soon forbidden to land their cargoes in Sierra Leone, except under extraordinary circumstances that seldom arose. MacCarthy was also suspicious of the first steps of the American Colonization Society to establish a base in what was to become Liberia, believing that the Society was merely a cloak to cover American schemes to plant a colony that would endanger British interests; he urgently pleaded for permission to seize the island of Sherbro and forestall the American peril. The British government refused, however, believing that the possibility of trouble with the United States outweighed any vague and unproved threat to Sierra Leone's revenues.[10]

Although American ships were forbidden the port, this did not mean that no American goods found their way into Sierra Leone. Shut out of Freetown, American traders resorted to smuggling (with the tacit approval and the wholehearted cooperation of local merchants and traders) and established themselves at the Los Islands. From there they undercut British trade in the Scarcies, Pongo, Nunez, Grande, and Sherbro rivers. Goods which were brought to Africa in American ships, and upon which no duties were ever paid, continued to flow into British territory, in spite of Governor MacCarthy. The actual smuggling of

---

[10] Fyfe, A History of Sierra Leone, p. 132; Brooks, pp. 98-100. The thoroughness of MacCarthy's exclusion of American shipping is shown by the fact that between 1817 and 1824 only six American ships, two of which were in distress and one of which was seized, entered the colony's port.

American goods to the rivers seems to have been done by British merchants who were already established on the Los Islands. To eliminate this nuisance and cut off the supply of American goods, MacCarthy seized the islands in 1818. Deprived of their island base, the Americans transferred their operations to the rivers, thus eliminating the British middlemen. In this way, the rivers (particularly the Nunez), which had been slaving centers, now became assembly and trading places for legitimate commerce in such products as ivory, dyewoods, and hides, even though the unhealthy river areas were still deadly places for white men through a large part of the year.[11]

Sierra Leone was finally opened to American shipping in 1831, but even then there was little legal American trade for a number of years. Because the duties on rum and tobacco, the two major American products, were prohibitive, American ships usually bypassed Freetown for more obscure places. Their goods still found their way into Sierra Leone, but by devious routes through the bush. Nevertheless, American trade seems to have been continuously prominent in the economic life of the colony, and it increased sharply after 1841. In 1849, with the final adoption of free trade principles by Great Britain, the ancient Navigation Laws were repealed, and American trade became so important on the West Coast that finally in 1852 an Order in Council made American money legal tender, along with British coinage.[12] American commercial enterprise in other parts of West Africa in the early nineteenth century followed a similar pattern.

Closely associated with Sierra Leone was the small British colony on the Gambia River. Great Britain had been forced to abandon

---

[11] Brooks, pp. 99-105, 112.

[12] N. A. W. Cox-George, Finance and Development in West Africa: The Sierra Leone Experience (London, 1961), p. 103. A shortage of currency forced Sierra Leone to allow other national coins to circulate as well.

the Gambia during the long period of wars with France and did not immediately move to reoccupy it at the end of the wars. Meanwhile, slavers, particularly Americans operating under the Spanish flag, were taking full advantage of the Gambia River as a favorable location for their activities. Consequently, in 1816 Governor MacCarthy led a force from Sierra Leone and hoisted the Union Jack over the island of Banjol, at the mouth of the river.[13] American shipping was speedily excluded from the Gambia. But, as in Sierra Leone, American legitimate traders merely became illegal traders--smugglers. Using the Cape Verde Islands as their base, they sold their illegal cargoes and took on, in increasing amounts, equally illegal African products. One American in particular, Samuel Hodges, Jr., from Massachusetts (as were nearly all American traders in Africa), built a trading post on São Tiago Island in 1818 and from there supplied the Gambia and the neighboring coastal areas with everything that was wanted.[14]

The British were finally forced by the demands of their own merchants to open the Gambia to American tobacco and lumber in 1824 so that the competition of the French merchants at Albreda could be met. American shipping and other American products were excluded until 1835, when such restrictions were abolished. From that time forward, legitimate and open American trade was important in the economic life of the colony. The volume of American business became so large that an American consul was assigned to Bathurst in 1834, and in 1851 Lieutenant Commander E.R. Thompson, of the U.S.S. Porpoise, reported that from thirty to forty American vessels touched there annually. In 1858 Daniel R. B. Upson, an American trader at Bathurst, informed the State Department that during the preceding year thirty-one

---

[13] Bella Sidney, Lady Southorn, The Gambia: The Story of the Groundnut Colony (London, 1952), pp. 153-155.

[14] Brooks, pp. 124-125.

American ships had entered the port and of the total imports of the colony ($569, 728) more than $70, 000 worth was in American goods.[15]

In the West African areas claimed by France, the story was quite similar to that of the British colonies--of futile efforts to enforce the old restrictions and to maintain a monopoly of both transportation and goods. The French government and its officials also found themselves unable to prevent a constant influx of American rum, lumber, tobacco, and cotton goods. The French, however, began to view the situation realistically somewhat in advance of the British, and in 1822 Gorée, in Senegal, was opened to the ships and products of all nations. An attempt was made to favor French ships by lowering the duties on goods that were carried in French holds, but this did not stop smuggling, and in 1852 Gorée was designated a free port. Other ports, such as Saint-Louis, in Senegal, were opened later, and mercantilism appeared dead on the African coast. For a number of years American traders and skippers seem almost to have dominated the commercial scene in West Africa.[16]

The outlines of American trade on the African coast south of

---

[15] E.J. Alagoa, "Preliminary Inventory of the Records of the United States Diplomatic and Consular Posts in West Africa, 1856-1935," _Journal of the Historical Society of Nigeria_, II, No. 1 (December, 1960), 78, 93; L.C. Howard, "American Involvement in Africa South of the Sahara, 1800-1860" (unpublished Ph.D. dissertation, Harvard University, 1956), pp. 98-100.

The share of American imports in the total of West African imports for selected years is given in Brooks, p. 243:

Year	Gambia	Sierra Leone	Gold Coast
1840	17%	5%	16% (1846)
1850	15	14	16
1860	28	12	41
1870	4	13	34

[16] In French West Africa the peak years were from 1865 to 1869. Brooks, p. 194.

Cape Palmas are quite similar to what has been described, with certain noteworthy differences. On the windward coast (north of Cape Palmas), trade was largely centered in a few places and carried on by a small number of merchants and traders. On the Ivory Coast, the Gold Coast, the Slave Coast, in the Gulf of Guinea and southward, trade was decentralized, with small quantities of goods at each trading point. A vessel would pick up a single tusk of ivory at one village, a few pieces of dyewood at another, a few measures of African pepper or a few hides at still another. A trader might take months in disposing of his cargo and accumulating one for his return voyage. This led to a commercial practice which seems to have been confined almost entirely to Americans. To save time, the Yankee trader would leave a quantity of trade goods at a coastal village, then sail to the next one, where more goods would be deposited. When the entire cargo had been landed, he retraced his route, picking up whatever had been left in trade at each village.[17]

As the British extended their control over most of the coastal areas on the Bight of Benin, they endeavored at first to apply the same restrictions that they had used in Sierra Leone. They enjoyed even less success, for there were no natural ports--no funnels--through which commerce had to flow and which could be watched and guarded with relative ease. Trading took place wherever a village lay within reach of the sea and the native boatmen could get through the surf. The geographical conditions that made this area a favored hunting ground for slaves also made it a profitable area for the trader with a small,

---

[17] Carneiro, "Memoir on the Trade to the West Coast of Africa Northward of the Equator," pp. 412-413. It is safe to say that if there had been any serious losses because of trusting the Africans, the Yankee trader would soon have discontinued the practice. This form of trade was reminiscent of the silent trade of the western Sudan mentioned in E.W. Bovill, The Golden Trade of the Moors (London, 1958).

handy vessel. The American trader became a familiar figure from Cape Palmas to Angola, with an occasional American ship going to Principe and São Tomé for coffee, dyewood, and palm oil.[18] Commander Joel Abbott, of the U.S.S. Decatur, Commanders Thomas Miller and William Tucker, of the Royal Navy, and John Carroll Brent, of the U.S.S. Jamestown, all gave reports of numerous American vessels trading up and down the coast, and the missionaries of of the American Board of Commissioners for Foreign Missions, establishing a mission at the mouth of the Gabon River in the early 1840's, were heartened by the frequent visits of American ships.[19]

When mercantilism was abandoned and free trade was introduced, American traders were able to push their wares and press their own interests with even greater ease. Americans had learned to cater to the tastes and needs of their African customers; they had a wide variety of goods to offer, usually at a lower price than that demanded by European competitors; their ships were reputed to load and unload faster than others. In the period from 1850 to the outbreak of the Civil War it seemed likely that Americans would dominate African commerce. European merchants and officials regarded them with dislike and apprehension, and many believed that American trade was the forerunner of annexation. An early instance was MacCarthy's suspicion of the settlement of Liberia. In the 1840's there was considerable fear in British circles that if the Gold Coast were abandoned (as the government in

---

[18] Brooks, pp. 177-178.

[19] Howard, "American Involvement in Africa South of the Sahara," p. 102; Miller, "Western Africa," pp. 296, 347; Brent, "Leaves from an African Journal," Knickerbocker Magazine, XXXIV (1850), 132; G.E. Metcalfe, Maclean of the Gold Coast: The Life and Times of George Maclean, 1801-1847 (London, 1962), p. 115; Missionary Herald, XLI (1845), 157.

London contemplated at one time), the Americans would step in and assume control.[20] American competition in trade, therefore, was a major reason in leading the British and French to pursue annexationist policies in parts of West and South Africa.

Although African commerce was a small part of United States commerce as a whole (less than 1 per cent), it was sufficiently important to receive special attention from the United States government, which sought to foster it by all possible means. Beginning with the appointment of an American consul at Cape Town in 1799, American consulates and commercial agencies were established at points along all of the West African coast. A consulate was established at Gambia in 1834; a consulate and commercial agency were established in Angola in the 1850's; and a commercial agent was appointed at Bissau in the same decade. Similar offices were established in other parts of Africa until by 1862 American interests in Africa were watched over by twenty-five consuls and agents.[21]

The American naval squadron that was stationed in West African waters from the early 1840's to the time of the Civil War to aid in suppressing the slave trade had another and almost equally important mission--the protection and furtherance of American commerce. Indeed, there are grounds for believing that in the minds of many officials in Washington this, and not the suppression of the slave trade, was the major reason for the squadron's existence. There was a real fear on the part of many Americans that the British would use the slave trade as an excuse and opportunity for eliminating all non-British trade on the African coast. American naval officers departing for the

---

[20] Brooks, p. 171.

[21] Howard, "American Involvement in Africa South of the Sahara," p. 103.

African station were invariably given instructions to prevent any interference, on any grounds, with legitimate American trade and shipping. The instructions of the Secretary of the Navy to Commodore Charles Skinner are illustrative: "The rights of our citizens engaged in lawful commerce are under the protection of our flag. And it is the chief purpose as well as the chief duty of our naval power to see that those rights are not improperly abridged or [violated]."[22]

Commodore Matthew C. Perry, who commanded the first American squadron stationed in West African waters (a result of the Webster-Ashburton Treaty of 1842), after forcibly breaking a boycott against American traders in certain native villages devoted considerable thought and attention to promoting American trade. As a result, he forwarded a lengthy letter to Washington, suggesting items to compose the cargo that could be profitably traded on the African coast. His list included the usual tobacco and cotton goods--he omitted rum--and such things as brown sugar, hams, cheese, crockery, tin buckets, ladies' shoes, gloves, paint, palm-leaf hats, brass kettles, paper and ink, ribbons for bonnets, silk stockings, sperm candles, and even "5 dozen cotton umbrellas."[23]

Eastern and Southern Africa

Simultaneously with the growth of American trade on Africa's West Coast, the ubiquitous and enterprising Yankee trader became even more prominent on the eastern side of the continent. In fact, for a time, the Yankee trader dominated the commerce and traffic of the western Indian Ocean.

---

[22] Quoted, ibid., pp. 117-118.

[23] Quoted in J.R. Spears, The American Slave-Trade (New York, 1900), pp. 42-43.

Although there was no regular trade between America and the East Coast of Africa during the colonial period, Americans were not complete strangers to the waters east of the Cape of Good Hope. One of the first recorded cargoes of slaves was brought to Massachusetts from Mozambique about 1680, and there were occasional cargoes from Madagascar (but the slave trade from East Africa never became particularly important). In addition to the possible whalers, slavers, and traders during the colonial era, in the seventeenth century numerous freebooters and pirates sailed from American ports for lawless strongholds in Madagascar and on the offshore islands of East Africa to prey on the rich trade of the Arabian Gulf and Red Sea.[24] Everyone who has reveled in pirate stories in his youth will recall that Captain Kidd sailed from New York. In 1698 the Earl of Bellomont, Royal Governor of New York, reported to the Lords of Trade and Plantations: "I find that those Pyrates that have given the greatest disturbance in the East Indies and Red Sea have either been fitted from New York or Rhode Island, and manned from New York."[25] During the Revolutionary War

---

[24] One of the founders of a pirate state called Libertalia, in northern Madagascar, was an American named Thomas Tew. After accumulating a dishonest fortune at sea, he returned to Rhode Island to live, but reverted to piracy and was finally killed somewhere in the Indian Ocean. A New York merchant named Frederic Phillips is said to have outfitted ships for slaving and piratical voyages to East Africa and to Madagascar and other Indian Ocean coasts and islands during the later years of the seventeenth century and the early part of the eighteenth, while Philadelphia merchants were also seeking a share of the business. See John Biddulph, _The Pirates of Malabar and an Englishwoman in India Two Hundred Years Ago_ (London, 1907), pp. 22-24, and A. Toussaint, "Early American Trade with Mauritius," _Essex Institute Historical Collections_, LXXXVII (1951), 373.

[25] Quoted in Foster Rhea Dulles, _The Old China Trade_ (Boston, 1930), p. 4. See also Biddulph, _The Pirates of Malabar_, pp. 38-68.

an adventurer calling himself Mauritius Augustus Count de Benyowski established a kingdom for himself in Madagascar. Driven out because of his brutual excesses, he went to Paris, where he favorably impressed no less a person than Benjamin Franklin. Benyowski then came to America to enlist aid, and finally returned to Madagascar in an American vessel. In 1786 the governor of the Ile de France (Mauritius) sent an expedition against him, and the adventurer was killed while resisting. Benyowski's following probably included at least a few Americans.[26]

Beyond doubt, the Americans who ventured into the Indian Ocean and along the eastern coast of Africa in pre-Revolutionary times included a due proportion of respectable traders. Unfortunately for the American historian, they sailed under the British flag, and, unlike the freebooters and cutthroats, they did not attract the special attention of the authorities. Consequently, they left no records. Such American voyages to the waters and places east of the Cape of Good Hope were, however, only occasional and sporadic, but after the Revolutionary War those waters and places became of direct interest and importance. Excluded from the West Indies--their major market in colonial times--American merchants and shipowners began searching the world for other and better markets. In 1783, Robert Morris, the so-called financier of the Revolution, wrote to John Jay: "I am sending some

---

[26] Memoirs and Travels of Mauritius Augustus Count de Benyowski, edited and with an Introduction by Captain S. Pasfield Oliver (London, 1904), pp. 456-620. Oliver says that Benyowski's objective was to establish a vast base for the slave trade (p. xix). See also Abbé Rochon, "A Voyage to Madagascar and the East Indies," in John Pinkerton (ed.), A General Collection of the Best and Most Interesting Voyages and Travels in All Parts of the World, XVI (London, 1814), 779-796, and George A. Shaw, Madagascar and France, with Some Account of the Island, Its People, Its Resources and Development (London, 1885), pp. 67-78.

ships to China in order to encourage in others the adventurous pursuit of commerce."[27] On Washington's birthday, 1784, the 360-ton Empress of China, sponsored by Morris and some other businessmen, slipped past Sandy Hook bearing a cargo intended to open the spice and silk lands of the Far East to the American merchant.

Morris was not alone in his hopes; while he was planning the voyage to China, several other merchants and shipowners were planning similar projects. In 1784 Christopher Champlin, of Newport, fitted a ship for an exploratory voyage to India, and Elias Hasket Derby, of Salem, dispatched one of his vessels on a similar mission to the Cape of Good Hope, the Guinea Coast, and thence to the West Indies.[28] And in that same commercially eventful year of 1784, on the day after Christmas, a ship flying a strange flag--one never before seen in Indian waters--dropped her anchor at Pondicherry. She was the United States, sailing from Philadelphia just a month after the Empress of China had left New York. Although the merchants and shipowners of Philadelphia have not attained the historical fame of their New England counterparts, in this instance they moved ahead of them and reached the goal first.

An unexpected development of these early voyages of commercial exploration was the sudden growth of American commerce with the Ile

---

[27] Quoted in Sydney and Marjorie Greenbie, Gold of Ophir; or, The Lure That Made America (Garden City, N.Y., 1925), p. 29.

[28] Massachusetts Historical Society, The Commerce of Rhode Island, 1726-1880 (Boston, 1914-1915), II, 200-206; Richard H. McKey, Jr., "Elias Hasket Derby and the Founding of the Eastern Trade," Essex Institute Historical Collections, XCVIII (1962), 1-25, 65-83. All of these ships were heavily armed, and sailed prepared for trouble. For instance, Derby's ship, the Grand Turk, carried twenty-two guns--an armament calculated to discourage pirates and ensure a friendly reception from natives. Derby's ships, incidentally, never engaged in the slave trade, in spite of voyaging to Guinea.

de France and the neighboring islands of the Mascarene group. The islands produced rich crops of tropical products, such as coffee, but did not grow sufficient foodstuffs for their fairly large European population. Moreover, during a long series of wars, French privateers in the Indian Ocean and East Indies usually sent their prizes to the Ile de France for condemnation and sale. The market was often glutted, and captors and prize courts were glad to sell their prizes for anything they would bring. Such a situation was meat and drink to the Yankee trader, who took full advantage of it.

The commercial possibilities of the Ile de France were first discovered by Derby, whose Grand Turk dropped anchor there in April, 1786, two years after her voyage to West Africa. Her cargo was quickly sold, and she was chartered by a French merchant for a voyage to Canton. Other American merchants followed Derby's lead, and the admiralty records of the island show that eighty-seven American ships anchored there between 1786 and 1793. An American merchant colony became an element in the population; in 1794 the United States government established a consulate. This was several years before an American consulate was established anywhere on the African continent. There were periods when relations were somewhat strained, as during the quasi war between the United States and France, but even that unhappy situation did not completely interrupt the commerce, or exclude the Yankee shipmaster-trader. Until the British captured the Ile de France in 1810 and added it to the British Empire, it was important in American foreign commerce and served admirably as an American commercial base in the Indian Ocean.[29]

---

[29] Toussaint, "Early American Trade with Mauritius," passim. See also Edwin B. Hewes, "Nathaniel Bowditch, Supercargo and Mariner," Essex Institute Historical Collections, LXX (1934), 210-217, and Jonathan Tucker, "The First Voyage to India from Salem, 1786-1787," Essex Institute Historical Collections, LXXV (1939), 44-45.

Because Indian trade was supposedly a tight monopoly of the East India Company, the Americans approached the shores of India with some misgivings, but their doubts were quickly dispelled. They were received hospitably, even by the company's officials. In 1788 the governor of Bengal, Lord Cornwallis (who had surrendered to Washington at Yorktown), commanded that American vessels should be treated as the "most favoured foreigners" at all of the company's settlements. In fact, one of the earliest American arrivals, the Chesapeake, of Baltimore, was granted exemption from customs duties by the Supreme Council of Bengal.[30]

With this somewhat unexpected encouragement, and with the profits accruing from the China trade, American shipping into the Indian Ocean increased rapidly. American trade received further stimulation by the Jay Treaty of 1794--a "Treaty of Amity, Commerce, and Navigation"--whereby commerce between the United States and India became entirely legal. The speed of the relatively small, handy American vessels, the safety to cargoes and passengers resulting from neutral status during the Napoleonic Wars, the shipmasters' willingness to connive at breaking certain British laws and their role as brokers for seized and confiscated goods all operated to the advantage of the American trade.[31]

After the first American ship anchored at the Cape of Good Hope in 1784, the number stopping there increased annually. Between

---

[30] Holden Furber, "The Beginnings of American Trade with India, 1784-1812," New England Quarterly, XI (1938), 241-242; William Milburn, Oriental Commerce (London, 1813), II, 136. Milburn, who was an official of the East India Company, credits the Chesapeake with being the first American ship to reach India, but it appears that the United States preceded her by several months.

[31] Americans were willing and ready to purchase prizes taken by the British as well as those taken by the French.

1795 and 1800 no less than one hundred and twenty-four vessels flying the American flag paid port charges at Cape Town. And this figure does not include American ships that avoided port charges by filling their water butts and buying fresh provisions at obscure and out-of-the-way places along the coast.[32]

South Africa quickly became an important point in American trade with the Far East and in the Indian Ocean. Many vessels stopped at Cape Town for water and provisions. What was more natural and logical than to include in the cargo materials that were salable in South Africa, and thus increase the profits of the voyage? Milburn, in his survey published in 1813, noted that "American ships frequently stop at the Cape on their outward voyage to China, to dispose of a part of their cargoes, consisting generally of lumber, for which they receive bills on India, or Spanish dollars." On the return voyage, the ship-master could top off his Chinese or Indian cargo with such South African products as wines (well known even then), ivory, hides, ostrich feathers, salt meats, or a score of items that commanded a ready sale in Europe or the West Indies.[33]

American shipping to the Far East and Africa was interrupted by the War of 1812, during which American ships, except for privateers and a few war vessels, vanished from the seas. But the traffic was resumed immediately after the Treaty of Ghent (1814), and not merely resumed--it expanded with almost explosive violence. As on the West Coast of Africa, the American trader and the American ship on the

---

[32] Eric Rosenthal, Stars and Stripes in Africa (London, 1938), p. 57.

[33] Milburn, Oriental Commerce, II, 48. In August, 1789, Hasket Derby, son of Elias Hasket Derby, stopping at Cape Town on a return voyage from Calcutta, sold $1,500 worth of Calcutta cloth and purchased 253 ostrich feathers. McKey, "Elias Hasket Derby and the Founding of the Eastern Trade," p. 24.

East Coast came almost invariably from New England and, more often than not, from the little port of Salem.

Boston took the lead in traffic with the Orient, but Salem was not too far behind. Boston ships often went around Cape Horn to the Northwest Coast of North America, where they loaded furs; thence they proceeded to China, and came home through the Indian Ocean. The Salem ships went out via the Cape of Good Hope, often avoiding Table Bay for fear of being wind-bound, touched at Madagascar or the Mascarenes, and then sailed on to Arabia and the East Indies. They returned by the same route, sometimes converging with ships from Boston.

Soon the Yankee trader was a familiar sight from the Cape of Good Hope to Cape Guardafui and at Madagascar and the offshore islands. Nathaniel Isaacs, an enterprising Anglo-Jewish trader, explorer, adventurer, and inadvertent empire builder, commenting upon a visit to an obscure port in 1831, said:

> The post of Lamoo [Lamu, Kenya] is free to all nations, but few have visited it, except the enterprising Americans, whose star-spangled banner may be seen streaming in the wind, where other nations, not even my own country, would not deign to traffic. America is the fore-runner of commerce in new countries, and she enjoys the sweets which they afford.[34]

The same keen observer, while at his home at St. Helena recovering from illness contracted in Africa, "became accidentally acquainted with an American captain, who commanded the ship Francis." The American plied everyone with questions about East Africa and spoke openly of his intention of making a trading voyage to that coast. Isaacs, irked by the supercilious treatment he had received from

---

[34] Nathaniel Isaacs, Travels and Adventures in Eastern Africa (Cape Town, 1936), II, 322. (Isaacs' work was published originally in 1836.)

British officialdom, answered him freely. "I cannot conceal that I felt this desire from the insufferable indifference we met with."[35] But, being a loyal British subject, Isaacs appealed strongly to his compatriots to annex Natal to the British Empire immediately, so that British traders could enter into "an advantageous traffic with those nations and tribes between Point Natal and the entrance to the Red Sea, with the islands in the Mozambique Channel, and with the Western Coast of Madagascar, now almost exclusively enjoyed by the Americans."[36]

Possibly even before American traders arrived on the East African coast, American whalers passed the Cape of Good Hope on their way into the Indian Ocean. They had ranged the West Coast since before the Revolutionary War, and a few years after the war they discovered that the waters surrounding Madagascar teemed with whales.[37] In 1795 Commodore Blankett, of the Royal Navy, reported the presence of American whalers along the South African coast, and in the same year, to the consternation of the Portuguese officials, a number of American whaling ships anchored in Delagoa Bay. By 1813 American whalers needing repairs were heaving down at a natural pier formed by the rocks at Saldanha Bay, not far from Cape Town.[38] In the early 1830's, Captain William F. Owen, of the Royal Navy, a noted explorer and indefatigable extender of the British Empire, reported that Delagoa Bay was "very much frequented" by both British and American whalers. Nathaniel Isaacs, upon one of his visits to the same place, saw "no

---

[35] Ibid., p. 5.

[36] Ibid., pp. 329-330. Emphasis added.

[37] Hohman, The American Whaleman, pp. 150, 230.

[38] Milburn, Oriental Commerce, I, 34; Alexander Starbuck, History of the American Whale Fishery (Waltham, Mass., 1878), p. 90.

less than eight American and one English whaling ships lying there, as well as an English brig and an American brigantine."[39]

As may be inferred from Isaacs' remarks about American enterprise and practical monopoly of the trade of the eastern coast of Africa, there was a certain degree of jealousy among the British (and other) competitors--a jealousy that was liberally seasoned with apprehension. The new nation across the Atlantic was commercially aggressive, and few businessmen or statesmen of the time could conceive of commercial aggressiveness without linking it with monopoly and territorial acquisition. The mercantilistic tradition of monopoly was still so strong that many men could see no other end than the complete elimination of all competitors, an objective which required territorial possession or, at least, a territorial base. If American ships in large numbers continued to enter the Indian Ocean and undercut British trade with the Orient, it was only a question of time until the Yankees would occupy territory from which they could eliminate all competition.

There were some Americans who favored the idea of an American settlement on the East African coast. In 1796 a ship from Boston, the *Hercules*, was wrecked at a point some five hundred miles northeast of Cape Town, near where the Indiaman *Grosvenor* had been wrecked fourteen years before. The ship's captain, Benjamin Stout, upon returning to the United States, addressed a memorial to the "President of the Continental Congress of the United States of America":

> I would draw the attention of the President to those commercial benefits which may be obtained by establishing a colony from America on that part of the coast where the ship was unfortunately wrecked.... A single settlement on the coast of Caffraria would amply repay its expense and the number of people necessary to the completion of

---

[39] Isaacs, *Travels and Adventures in Eastern Africa*, II, 283.

such an undertaking might be limited to 1,000.[40]

Very early in the history of American traffic to and through South Africa, British officials began to worry about ultimate American intentions. In 1800 Sir George Yonge, the governor at Cape Town, informed London that American trade with China and the East Indies was increasing rapidly and was entirely dependent upon supplies and services available in the Cape Colony. Implicit in his report was the belief that the Americans would not want to remain dependent indefinitely upon a foreign power for the continuation of their new commerce--sooner or later they would have to have their own base or bases. Yonge added, to give point to his statement: "Here have been many fine American ships since my arrival and here is now a fine American frigate of 32 guns [the Essex] and another expected, sent to protect the American commerce in India, which has been much harassed by French privateers fitted out at the Mauritius." Moreover, he said, the newly arrived American consul had informed him that the United States was fitting out fifteen frigates and five seventy-fours (ships of war carrying seventy-four guns) to operate against the French.[41]

After the War of 1812, when large numbers of American ships again appeared in the Indian Ocean, British officials, settlers, and traders in southern Africa became increasingly uneasy about

---

[40] Quoted in Eric Rosenthal, Stars and Stripes in Africa (London, G. Routledge, 1938), p. 92; see also J.N. Reynolds, Voyage of the United States Frigate Potomac, under the Command of Commodore John Downes, during the Circumnavigation of the Globe, in the Years 1831, 1832, 1833, and 1834 (New York, 1835), pp. 82-83. Captain Stout praised the Africans highly for the hospitality and help they extended to him and his crew after the wreck.

[41] Quotation from Rosenthal, Stars and Stripes in Africa, p. 93. See also Edgar Stanton Maclay, A History of the United States Navy from 1775 to 1893 (New York, 1894-1895), I, 192, and "Extract of Capt. E. Preble's Journal on Board the Essex," Essex Institute Historical Collections, X, Part III (1869), 66-69.

American intentions. Reflecting an important segment of British opinion, the London Times urged emigration from Britain and other measures to solve pressing problems at home and at the same time forestall American ambitions in Africa: "Make the Cape a free port... and we banish North America from the India seas." And Captain Owen, of the Royal Navy, reported to his superiors in London that "should the Bay [Delagoa Bay] fall into the possession of either the French, American, or the Russian, it would be most ruinous not only to our colony, but to our East India possessions and commerce."[42]

Today such fears are patently absurd, but to the British colonials of the 1830's the American peril seemed very real. Dr. John Philip, the superintendent in South Africa for the London Missionary Society, visualized Americans from Delagoa Bay arming the natives and re-enacting on the South African frontier the horrors that had occurred on the frontiers in America. Nathaniel Isaacs, because of his open friendship with Americans, was accused of being secretly a "United States consul," with the mission of training the natives in the use of firearms. And in spite of this accusation (of which he was probably ignorant), Isaacs vehemently urged the governor of Cape Colony to annex Natal before the Americans could do so. That responsible British colonial officials took the American peril seriously is attested by a letter which the governor at Cape Town wrote to the Colonial Office in 1831: "With reference to . . . the possibility of the United States forming a settlement [in Natal], it is hardly necessary to remark how embarrassing such neighbours might actually prove to this Colony." In 1834, a large group of British merchants and settlers in the Cape Colony sent a petition to London urging the immediate annexation of Natal. In proof of the urgency of the situation, Dr. Andrew Smith, a well-known medical officer who had visited Natal in 1832,

---

[42] Quotations from Rosenthal, Stars and Stripes in Africa, pp. 93-94.

wrote that the "belief [in American designs in Natal] has lately gained ground from the circumstance of an American vessel of war, with a political commissioner on board, having run along the coast and observed the situation....Let the intention of the Government be what it may, we know from undoubted authority that the nation [the United States] is about to send out missionaries to labour in that vicinity."[43]

Despite the fact that the United States took no action in the still unclaimed territory of Natal and that the Portuguese officials still dozed undisturbed at Delagoa Bay, British suspicion of American intentions lingered for years. The fear that American traders and ships on the coast and in East African waters were forerunners of American annexation quite probably helped stimulate the government in London finally, in 1843, to consent to adding Natal formally to the British Empire.

During the period of excitement over the possibility of an American colony in South Africa, the fears of British officialdom and British colonists could not have been allayed by two Salem Yankees, Jonathan Lambert and Richard Cleveland, who took possession of the then unoccupied island of Tristan da Cunha, in the South Atlantic not far from St. Helena and only a few hundred miles from the Cape. Lambert and Cleveland attempted to establish a colony there. Their

[43] Quotation from the governor's letter is in Rosenthal, Stars and Stripes in Africa, p. 97; Dr. Smith's letter is in Harold Graham Mackeurtan, The Cradle Days of Natal (1497-1845) (London, 1930), p. 329. Dr. Smith's prediction seemed partly fulfilled by the arrival, in 1835, of a group of American missionaries who came in response to an invitation from the same Dr. Philip who, ten years before, had been in terror of the American peril. The earnest, devoted men of the missionary group, who were destined to achieve an honorable place in South African history, would have been shocked if they had known that they were feared as political agents--as spies and what the present age calls "fifth columnists." The warship mentioned was the U.S.S. Peacock, carrying an envoy from President Andrew Jackson to negotiate commercial treaties with the Sultan of Muscat and other Eastern potentates.

intentions were not at all imperialistic--they hoped to turn a profit by selling fresh provisions to the Indiamen, whose usual course took them close to the island. The two adventurers even offered to place their bit of pre-empted real estate under British authority in return for aid from the Cape. A few months after they had established themselves, a British visitor reported flourishing fields and gardens and urged the governor of Cape Colony to annex the island, along with its settlers. Although the Americans planted corn, potatoes, pumpkins, onions, and other garden truck and slaughtered sea elephants to render a large quantity of oil, they were unable to attract enough customers or colonists to make the scheme a success, and eventually they had to admit defeat.[44]

There can be little question that an American base in southeastern Africa would have facilitated American commerce in the Indian Ocean, but without doubt the last thing the United States government wanted was to become territorially involved in Africa. The American people as a whole would not have supported any annexation of territory outside North America, no matter how much the merchants of the Atlantic seaboard might desire it. Nor did the suddenly flourishing trade with Zanzibar and other African dominions of the Sultan of Muscat change the government's mind.

The American sloop of war Peacock, sailing up the African coast in 1832 on a commercial mission to Muscat and other Eastern principalities, constituted a recognition by Washington of what had rather quickly become an accomplished fact--a growing and highly lucrative trade with Zanzibar.

---

[44]Herbert M. Bratter, "Jonathan Lambert of Salem, the Yankee Who Would Be King," Essex Institute Historical Collections, LXXXVIII (1952), 150-162; Edwin B. Hewes, "Jonathan Lambert of Salem, King of Tristan D'Acunha," Essex Institute Historical Collections, LXXI (1935), 1-6; Captain Benjamin Morrell, A Narrative of Four Voyages (New York, 1832), pp. 354-355; Benjamin Seaver, "Mr. Seaver's Letter concerning the Islands of Tristan D'Acunha," Historical Collections of the Massachusetts Historical Society, Ser. 2, II (1814), 125-128. Seaver, who was the British visitor referred to above, said that there were three Americans on the island, although he named only Lambert.

and the East Coast of Africa. It is quite probable that American whalers and occasional traders touched at Zanzibar early in the century, but one of the first American vessels of which there is any record was the brig Laurel, of Salem, which presumably anchored there in 1825. The following year the Virginia, also of Salem, spent eighteen days at Zanzibar and sailed directly for home with a cargo that included "117 elephant's teeth"--the first vessel to sail directly from Zanzibar to Salem.[45] The commerce thus opened grew rapidly. Three more Salem vessels arrived at Zanzibar in 1826, and in the following year seven American ships, most of them from Salem, anchored there.

Most significant for the future of American trade and American relations with East Africa was the Mary Ann, of New Bedford, with a cargo consigned to Edmund Roberts. Roberts, although still a young man, already had a wide mercantile and quasi-diplomatic experience. Having recently suffered financial losses, he decided that the virgin trading field of Zanzibar and East Africa would be a good place to recoup. With borrowed capital, he chartered the Mary Ann and sailed on June 10, 1827. On arriving at Zanzibar, he was extremely annoyed by the delays put in his way by the local Arab officials and by what he regarded as their discrimination in favor of the British. Only British merchants were permitted to trade freely at Zanzibar; all others had to deal through local agents who frequently overcharged, substituted unwanted goods, and seized upon all sorts of opportunities to line their

---

[45] Norman Robert Bennett, "Americans in Zanzibar, 1825-1845," Essex Institute Historical Collections, XCV (1959), 240-242. It had been supposed, before the publication of Bennett's studies, that the first American vessels at Zanzibar were the Ann and the Spy, in 1826. A booklet on sailing directions for the East African coast, compiled by Amos Lefavour, Jr., in the collection of the Beverly (Massachusetts) Historical Society, notes that a Captain Johnson visited Zanzibar in 1823.

own pockets. Such practices threatened any prospect of a promising American trade. Consequently, in January, 1828, when the Sultan of Muscat, who was also sovereign of Zanzibar, visited that African island, Roberts obtained an audience and complained vigorously about the agents and the special privileges accorded the British. The Sultan listened sympathetically to Roberts' complaints. He was interested in obtaining American munitions to use against his old enemies, the Portuguese (as well as his rebellious African subjects on the mainland), and he saw in American trade an opportunity to free himself from complete dependence upon Europeans. Hence, the Sultan not only welcomed Roberts and gave orders for immediate relief from the difficulties he had encountered, but went even further and suggested a commercial treaty between the United States and his own government.[46]

Roberts returned to the United States and lost no time in imparting the information to his old friend Levi Woodbury, Secretary of the Navy and former senator from New Hampshire. As a result, Roberts was appointed a special commissioner empowered by President Jackson to negotiate commercial treaties with the Sultan of Muscat, the King of Siam, and "such Asiatic potentates, as he might find favourably disposed." He was ordered to keep his mission secret from the European powers, and in dealing with Oriental rulers he was enjoined to distinguish the United States from the European countries by stressing its "non-imperial character." Roberts sailed from the United States on his commercial-diplomatic mission early in 1832 on board the U.S.S. Peacock. To maintain secrecy, his nominal status was merely that of ship's clerk, but the secret was evidently not kept well,

---

[46] C.T. Brady, Commerce and Conquest in East Africa (Salem, 1950), pp. 89-90; W.S.W. Ruschenberger, A Voyage round the World, Including an Embassy to Muscat and Siam in 1835, 1836, and 1837 (Philadelphia, 1838), pp. 10-11.

as shown by the fact, mentioned earlier, that in South Africa a "political commissioner" was known to be on board.

The *Peacock* arrived at Muscat in September, 1833, after some misadventures upon an uncharted reef on the Arabian coast. Roberts was warmly welcomed by Sultan Seyyid Said, who was flattered to be treated as an equal by the President of a great country. He saw the opportunity for an expansion of trade for his dominions, increased wealth for himself, and a new political friendship that might be of value some day against the dominant power of Great Britain. Furthermore, he was having difficulty in subduing a rebellion at Mombasa and was glad to get aid from any source. The negotiations took only three days, and on September 21, 1833, a treaty was signed by the Sultan and by Roberts as the authorized representative of the President.

The Sultan was more than generous in the terms which he conceded. Americans were placed on the same status as "the nation most favored," a provision which gave them equality with the British. Americans were granted full authority to travel and trade without restriction in all parts of the Sultan's dominions, to arrive and depart without hindrance, and were to be charged not more than a five per cent impost on cargoes actually landed. The United States was authorized to establish consulates at the principal commercial centers (i.e., at Zanzibar itself), with full diplomatic immunity and protection for the consuls. The consuls, moreover, were to have full and exclusive jurisdiction over disputes between Americans. The Sultan agreed further to return shipwrecked American seamen without compensation, and, outside the treaty, he voluntarily undertook at once to recover the guns and anchors that had been jettisoned from the *Peacock* when she struck the reef just before her arrival at Muscat. The sole restriction in the treaty was a curious provision that at Zanzibar munitions were to be sold only to the Sultan's government; elsewhere in his domains "the said munitions of war" could be "freely sold without any restrictions whatever to the highest bidder."

In return for all this, the United States granted the Sultan's subjects and ships the rights of the most-favored nation if they should ever land in America--not a particularly important concession, as the Sultan knew. But in spite of the apparent inequality, the Sultan was very happy with the agreement and sent President Jackson a glowing letter full of Oriental rhetoric and promises of enduring good will. Upon Roberts' return to the United States, the Senate promptly approved the treaty, and he was again dispatched on the Peacock to exchange ratifications, a mission which he completed on September 30, 1835.[47]

During the negotiations the Sultan offered to allow American settlements to be made on the African mainland, if the United States would assist him in suppressing the rebellion at Mombasa. The offer was, of course, declined, but it seems to have come to the ears of the suspicious and watchful British. Combined with the presence of an American war vessel--the Peacock had touched at Zanzibar on the way to Muscat--and the recent arrival of American missionaries in Natal, the offer seemed to justify the fears of the British regarding American intentions in Africa. Lord Palmerston is supposed to have pooh-poohed the idea; nevertheless, in 1834 a British warship was dispatched to Zanzibar, and, as already brought out, Englishmen remained nervous about the "American peril" for years to come.

The real threat to British interests came not from the United States government, but from American traders and whalers, particularly from the Salem merchants and traders--almost the only Americans who were interested in East Africa at all. While Roberts was negotiating the commercial treaty with the Sultan, the Salem men were making every effort to secure the East African trade for themselves. Their near monopoly was such that of the thirty-two American vessels touching at Zanzibar between September, 1832, and May, 1834, twenty were

---

[47] Ruschenberger, A Voyage round the World, pp. 89-94.

from Salem. During the same period, only nine vessels from European nations entered the port.[48]

The Salem men tried at first to keep the Zanzibar trade a secret within their own group. Failing in this, they acted swiftly, as soon as the news of Roberts' treaty became generally known, to make sure that the consul at Zanzibar would be from Salem. Largely through the efforts and lobbying of the merchants John Bertram and Michael Shepard, the man appointed was Richard P. Waters, of Salem.[49]

Waters arrived at Zanzibar and assumed his duties on March 17, 1837. He was accorded a cordial welcome by the Sultan, who also gave him his choice of any house in the city, rent free, for his consulate. Waters had been warned by the State Department not to take advantage of the unusual privileges he enjoyed under the treaty, but in those days a United States consul was never a career man. A consul's official salary and fees were hardly enough to pay for his groceries, and it was taken for granted that he was also in business, either for himself or as a representative of some business concern.

Waters crossed swords almost at once with the Master of the Custom House, one Jairam Sewji (or Jeram Sewejee), who was paying large sums for his office and fully intended to make a profit. In addition to other practices, Jairam had devised a simple and effective system of extortion from local merchants who sold goods to Americans, so as to compensate himself for the loss of the export duty which he had collected before the treaty. He required Americans who purchased goods to bring them to the customhouse; even though he could not collect any duty, he controlled the hiring of coolies to transport the goods. And for reasons which are not clear, Waters quarreled also with native merchants. The result was that, initially, he was quite unpopular.

---

[48] Brady, Commerce and Conquest in East Africa, p. 98.

[49] Bennett, "Americans in Zanzibar," p. 250.

But after an unpropitious beginning, the atmosphere cleared for the American consul, and his relationships became cordial. He and Jairam apparently decided that they could realize greater profits by cooperation than by competition, and they formed a quiet alliance that enabled them to dominate the commerce of Zanzibar. The rival British trading firm of Newman, Hunt and Christopher, finding itself operating at an annual loss, gave up the fight and left Zanzibar. Jairam, in his position as Master of the Custom House, could block (or, at least, make very difficult) any transaction which Waters did not approve. In return for this cooperation, Jairam became the unofficial middleman for the Salem merchants, determining what was to be sold, to whom, and at what price. Both Waters and Jairam received a commission on each transaction, and it appears that Waters was also actively engaged in business for himself, as well as for the Salem merchants whom he represented.

Naturally, such a system did not appeal to those who were on the outside. Not only was the Zanzibar trade dominated by Salem merchants; it was also a monopoly in the hands of a small group determined to keep out all competitors. The British government in 1841 designated a consul for the first time, in an effort to protect British commercial and political interests. By February, 1842, Her Majesty's representative was able to report that British subjects now had equal rights with Americans in the Zanzibar trade--a reversal of the situation of a few years before.[50]

In spite of his devotion to his own interests, Waters was a most capable and efficient consular representative of his country. Although Salem was unable to maintain a monopoly of the Zanzibar trade,

---

[50] Ibid., pp. 254-255. It is amusing to note that this first British consul, Captain Atkins Hamerton, complained that at his initial audience with the Sultan the latter was flanked on each side by a picture of a British warship surrendering to an American.

Americans continued to dominate it until the Civil War, and the foundations of this commercial pre-eminence were firmly laid by Waters. His commercial ethics were those of his times, and he did nothing that his competitors would not have done, given the opportunity. He left Zanzibar a very wealthy man, and his erstwhile enemy and later ally, Jairam Sewji, is said to have realized $100,000 annually from his position as Master of the Custom House.

The treaty between the Sultan and the United States provided for most-favored-nation treatment of Zanzibar vessels in the ports of the United States. American officials and the public were astonished when, on April 30, 1840, a bark flying the scarlet Zanzibar ensign dropped anchor in New York harbor. Owned by the Sultan himself, she was the al-Sultanah, commanded by Ahmad bin Na'aman, one of the Sultan's high officials, and laden with a valuable cargo upon which His Highness hoped to reap a profit. She carried also a special representative on a mission of commerce and good will, who brought two Arabian horses and other princely gifts for President Van Buren. After several weeks in New York, during which Ahmad bin Na'aman and his crew were lionized and feted and the ship was repaired and put into sailing condition at the New York navy yard, the al-Sultanah put to sea on her return voyage. Commercially, the voyage was a moderate success; diplomatically, it was a great success. In the somewhat confused relationships of the next few years Ahmad bin Na'aman was the leader of what the British consul at Zanzibar bitterly called the "American Party."[51]

During the prosperous years before the Civil War the American firms, led by Bertram-Shepard of Salem, known as the "Big Firm," built a large trading complex embracing the whole East African coast,

---

[51] Hermann Frederick Eilts, "Ahmad bin Na'aman's Mission to the United States in 1840: The Voyage of Al-Sultanah to New York City," Essex Institute Historical Collections, XCVIII (1962), 219-277.

the offshore islands, and Arabia. Determined to expand their trade in the face of increasing competition from Europeans, the leading American trading companies soon had agents in Madagascar, Mozambique, Muscat, and Aden. By the middle of the nineteenth century they held a commanding lead in the commerce of the East African littoral. After Waters' departure, Jairam worked with various American merchants and even helped them when they were in need. During the Mexican War (1846-1848), when American merchants had difficulty in obtaining specie, Jairam lent them what they required so as to keep them in business.

But the American insiders, in spite of their influence, were not without competition. In 1849 the famous Hamburg firm of William O'Swald and Company opened a branch in Zanzibar with the avowed intention of making themselves the leading traders on the island. Nor was the competition limited to Europeans. Ahmad bin Na'aman's voyage to New York had been undertaken despite the quiet but determined opposition of Waters and the Salem merchants and as a direct result of representations made by New York merchants who wanted to break into the dominance of Salem.[52] In 1852 Rufus Green and Company of Providence began trading in Zanzibar and quickly became leading competitors of the Salem men. Although none of the newcomers succeeded in displacing the old, well-established Salem firms, their competition drove prices to new heights, thereby reducing profits and forcing merchants to extend their activities to other East African and Arabian ports to assure full cargoes for their ships.

Unfortunately, while American trade flourished at mid-century, diplomatic relations between the United States and the Sultan deteriorated, with numerous petty disputes between Charles Ward, the American consul, and the Sultan. First, there was an altercation over the status of of the Indians of Zanzibar, who alternately claimed to be subjects of the

---

[52] Ibid., pp. 234-235.

Sultan and the British Queen, whichever was more convenient at the moment. As subjects of the Sultan, they could trade on the coast; as British subjects, they could claim the protection of Great Britain when they were threatened by foreign commercial firms. After a protracted dispute, the Sultan, much to Ward's disgust, accepted the interpretation of the British consul, that Indians were British subjects.

Other questions exacerbated Zanzibar-United States relations for a time. The Sultan threatened to carry on direct trade with the United States, as he had done on a limited scale with the voyage of the al-Sultanah. Since this would undercut American firms and traders, the threat caused considerable alarm. Then, too, in spite of the clear provisions of Roberts' treaty, the Sultan refused to grant formal permission for Americans to trade in his dominions on the mainland. Ill feeling was intensified when Ward helped an American sailor to flee the island after conviction by a Zanzibari court. The series of disputes reached a climax on July 4, 1850, when the Sultan refused to permit a public salute to the American flag. Ward demanded a written apology and, when it was not forthcoming, indignantly closed the consulate and left Zanzibar. Upon arriving in Washington, he advised the State Department to use force in recovering American honor. The department had received similar advice from other quarters, and on December 2, 1851, the U.S.S. Susquehanna anchored at Zanzibar; her commander, John Aulick, served an ultimatum: he would bombard the town unless the required apology was made immediately. The Sultan's governor acquiesced, American honor was satisfied, and the whole unfortunate affair was soon forgotten. A new consul, John F. Webb, quickly reestablished the former friendly relations, and no new causes of discord arose to mar them.

American domination of the Zanzibar and East African trade ended with the Civil War. American cotton goods were unobtainable for several years, and the United States ceased to export firearms and gunpowder. Americans were forced to seek new goods to sell. They shipped cargoes of soap and codfish, but neither of these products was in great demand at Zanzibar. They managed to get American gold accepted at par and worked up something of a market for that commodity, but gold could not possibly fill the holds of ships or take the place of other items. Some among the American merchants even imported cotton goods from England, simply to fulfill their contracts and hold their customers. Often their purchases had to be transported to America in British vessels. American credit was maintained at a high level, and the American merchants hoped to regain their lost ground when the war ended, but the gains made by British, German, and Indian traders at American expense could not be overcome entirely. In 1859, in both tonnage and the number of ships entering the port, Americans had exceeded the British, Germans, and French combined; in 1866 they were surpassed by each of these and in 1871 were still lagging behind.

During the years of American pre-eminence in nineteenth-century African trade, the dominance of Salem on both coasts was striking. Enterprising merchants of the Massachusetts town took the lead in opening trade with Africa, and throughout the era of direct commerce between the United States and Africa, they provided by far the greater part of the cargoes, and, further, the cargoes were carried in vessels owned, manned, and usually built at Salem. The Yankee trader living and conducting business on the African coast was, more often than not, a man from Salem. As early as 1798 a Salem vessel sailed for Mocha, in the Red Sea, a voyage which brought her to the shores of Africa; by 1805, no less than forty-eight Salem ships had "gone round the Cape."[53] A few years later, of a total of seventy-three

---

[53] Winthrop L. Marvin, The American Merchant Marine: Its History and Romance from 1620 to 1902 (New York, 1902), p. 202.

American vessels known to have been in the waters of Madagascar and eastern Africa between 1824 and 1837, sixty-three were from Salem; of the remainder, several were Salem vessels chartered by merchants of other cities.[54] On the West Coast, Commander Joel Abbott, of the U.S.S. Decatur, reported in 1844 that there was a large trading factory at Ambriz (Angola) maintained by a group of Salem merchants and that eight or ten ships, mostly from Salem, visited that part of the African coast regularly.[55] A Salem trading house also had a permanent representative at Luanda.[56] In the fiscal year ending June 30, 1860, twenty-six vessels from West Africa and eight from East Africa docked at Salem. In 1857 thirty-two ships from Africa entered the port, as compared with fifteen at Boston. The ships arriving at this single port in 1860 paid duties amounting to $36,739--a large sum for those days.[57]

Salem's position in African commerce was partly the result of a natural accident--its small and shallow harbor could not accommodate large vessels.[58] Hence, Salem ships were in general small, with light draft, and much better suited to the dangerous waters of Africa than the bigger, less maneuverable craft typically built and owned by

---

[54] Bennett, "Americans in Zanzibar," pp. 260-262.

[55] Howard, "American Involvement in Africa South of the Sahara," p. 102.

[56] "Letters from David Livingstone, the Distinguished African Explorer, Written in 1856," Essex Institute Historical Collections, XII (1874), 285.

[57] Samuel Eliot Morison, The Maritime History of Massachusetts, 1783-1860 (Boston, 1921), p. 377; Robert Greenhalgh Albion, "From Sails to Spindles: Essex County in Transition," Essex Institute Historical Collections, XCV (1959), 119.

[58] Charles E. Cartwright, The Tale of Our Merchant Ships (New York, 1924), p. 123. Ships drawing more than twelve feet could not dock there.

the merchants of Boston, New York, or Philadelphia. There were few harbors worthy of the name along the African coast. The innumerable sand bars, high surf, occasional tornadoes, and dry, sandy harmattan from the Sahara constituted perils that the light, handy schooner or brig from Salem could "claw out of," while a bigger ship might come to disaster. Consequently, the merchants of the larger cities chose to trade in regions where natural dangers were less forbidding, leaving African commerce to the "poor relations" at Salem. Conversely, although the merchants of Salem sent vessels to India, China, and the Spice Islands, there they were handicapped in their competition with Boston and New York; Africa they had to themselves, and a very good thing they made of it.

From America the Salem ships carried a wide variety of goods wanted and needed in Africa: tobacco, rum, lumber, brown sugar, hams, cheese, crockery, sperm candles, tin buckets, brass kettles, bonnet ribbons, gloves, ladies' shoes, and cotton umbrellas. Besides these articles, traders found a ready market for brass wire, beads, gunpowder, muskets, and scores of other articles.

Probably foremost among the goods wanted from America, especially in East Africa, was coarse, strong cotton cloth. Cloth manufactured in Massachusetts for the African trade proved to be superior to the products of Manchester and Madras for the African's needs and purposes. Over wide regions in East Africa, American-made cloth became the standard of trade, even the circulating medium, used instead of money. The work "merikani" passed into the languages of the region, and it remains to this day, although present-day merikani is made in Manchester or Osaka.[59] For the ivory hunter a stout, heavy, sharp hatchet was as necessary a part of his equipment as his gun,

---

[59] Kenneth Ingham, A History of East Africa (London, 1962), pp. 71-73.

and the best hatchets came from America: "Even sixty or seventy years ago, the old-time hunters tell us, they used 'superior American hatchets.'"[60]

To pay for ivory and other purchases, American ships brought to Zanzibar wooden boxes packed with "Zanzibar dollars," minted in America. The near extermination of the elephant in western Africa made East Africa the primary source of ivory. With the growing population and wealth of the United States, ivory for piano and organ keys, billiard balls, knife handles, and various other uses came into wide demand.[61] One is likely to visualize ships returning from exotic, faraway countries as laden with exotic products, "ivory, and apes, and peacocks," with incense, jewels, and spices, but the small bulk of ivory and specie could not nearly fill the holds of the ships sailing back to America. To render a voyage profitable it was necessary to return with other, more readily obtainable articles. Commander Thomas Miller, of the Royal Navy, urging his compatriots to extend their West African commerce, mentioned palm oil, beeswax, dyewood, orchilla weed (archil), white and yellow gum, and copper ore, in addition to ivory.[62] Hides, required in enormous quantities by the expanding shoe and leather industries of New England, became one of the leading articles of import into the United States, from Africa and anywhere else where they might be obtained. A government report of 1855 shows that hides were a major import from Africa, being exceeded in value

---

[60] Ernst D. Moore, Ivory, Scourge of Africa (New York, 1931), pp. 211-212.

[61] Ibid., passim.

[62] Miller, "Western Africa," p. 296.

only by the more commonly known ivory and palm oil.[63]

Throughout most of the nineteenth century and before the rise of the mineral oil industry, the machinery of the new industrialism was kept operating smoothly by an African product, palm oil. In addition, the increasing trend toward personal cleanliness and sanitation called for vast quantities of groundnuts and palm oil for the manufacture of soap. The wastes from farm and slaughterhouse no longer provided enough material--it was necessary to call on Africa to fill the need.

Before the rise of the chemical industry and the introduction of synthetic dyes, dyewoods were an important article of commerce, and Africa was especially rich in woods from which dyes could be extracted. Cabinet woods, too, were needed by American craftsmen who were building fine houses for wealthy merchants and constructing elegant furniture to fill those houses. Once again, Africa was a prolific source. The Yankee schooner or brig, laboring homeward with her hold crammed, was likely to have rough logs lashed as deckload, wherever room could be found for them.

One major American product, and possibly the most profitable of all to the merchants of Salem, remains to be mentioned. Gum copal, the base for fine varnishes and lacquers, is found in many parts of Africa, but the arid highlands of East Africa proved to be the world's most important source. At first its use involved considerable difficulty, but in 1835, Jonathan Whipple, of Salem, invented a new and cheap process for cleaning the gum and preparing it for use, thereby adding

---

[63] Report of the Secretary of the Treasury, Transmitting a Report from the Register of the Treasury, of the Commerce and Navigation of the United States for the Year Ending June 30, 1855 (Washington, 1855), pp. 223, 241. It may be recalled that the brig Pilgrim, on the voyage immortalized by Richard Henry Dana, Jr., in Two Years before the Mast, sailed around the Horn to California to obtain a cargo of hides.

to the firmness of Salem's hold on East African trade and contributing to its continuing prosperity. Varnishes and lacquers used throughout the United States were made from gum copal received from Africa through Salem.[64]

Thus, for several decades, there was a procession of small ships across the Atlantic and down the length of that ocean, past the Cape of Good Hope and into the Indian Ocean, bearing lumber, tobacco, cloth, rum, hatchets, muskets, gunpowder, chinaware, brass wire, beads, and scores of other articles.On the return voyage to America they were heavy-laden with gum copal, ivory, hides, guano, cloves, senna, ebony, or whatever else the shrewd Yankee skipper recognized as a possible source of profit. Yankee traders and skippers contributed notably to making the rest of the world aware of Africa and to bringing it into the orbit of world affairs.

The decrease in direct American trade with Africa after the Civil War can be ascribed to a number of causes. Probably the foremost was a general decline in the American merchant marine owing to the depredations of Confederate cruisers in the Civil War, a lessening of interest in foreign commerce, and the concentration of the American people (including many New England merchants) on the development and exploitation of their own Far West. Next, or equally important, was the transition from sail to steam as motive power for ships--steamships could transport bigger cargoes farther and faster. When the steamship took over the task of carrying the world's goods on the oceans, Salem was doomed as a major port. Its harbor could not accommodate steam vessels large enough to compete with those visiting Africa from Germany and Great Britain. The small Yankee trading vessel, moreover, which could be operated in competition with other sailing craft,

---

[64] Howard, "American Involvement in Africa South of the Sahara," p. 166.

was unable to hold its own against the faster service and lower relative operating cost of the steam-powered ship. The Stars and Stripes practically vanished from the coasts of Africa; the Salem trader was replaced by a trader from Hamburg or Liverpool.[65] And, finally, the partition of Africa, under which European powers established sovereignty over Africa, also hurt the American traders. The colonial powers and their shipping conferences tended to discriminate against foreign shippers and traders.

II. MISSIONARIES AND COLONIZATION SOCIETIES

A feature of the life and thought of the nineteenth century that deeply affected the impact of America and Africa upon each other grew out of the religious revival that had started in the eighteenth century. In Europe the revival, closely interwoven with the Industrial Revolution, produced social reforms and afforded help for the disinherited peasants who swarmed into the slums of Manchester and Lille. In America, the revival was one of the main sources of the abolition movement, and in both Europe and America it led directly to the nineteenth-century missionary movement. Sincere Christians were anxious for the salvation of the heathen, wherever they might be. The English Methodists organized a regular system of foreign missions in 1787, and in 1795 the London Missionary Society was founded and immediately started work in the Far East. The various evangelical and Protestant bodies of the Continental countries soon joined the missionary movement; the idea

---

[65] Numerous examples show that steamships were cutting deeply into the business of sailing-ship owners during the 1870's and 1880's; see Norman R. Bennett, "William H. Hathorne, Merchant and Consul in Zanzibar," Essex Institute Historical Collections, XCIX (1963), 125, 132, 134.

quickly took root in the United States. The nineteenth century became the greatest era of missionary effort since the early days of Christianity, as missionaries from Europe and America extended their activities into Asia, Africa, and even the tiny islands of the South Seas.

Widespread interest in Africa was stimulated by the formation of the Association for Promoting the Discovery of the Interior Parts of Africa in 1788 and by the rise of antislavery sentiment in the Western world. This interest served to direct religious and philanthropic attention to the Dark Continent. Closely interlocked with religious and philanthropic interest were the movements to abolish the slave trade and provide for the welfare of free Negroes and slaves rescued from the slavers.

By 1815 the slave trade was no longer a respectable business. This change took place in the United States largely because of the antislavery movement in Great Britain. In 1772, reversing earlier rulings of the British courts, Justice Mansfield declared unequivocally that "the claim of slavery [in Great Britain] can never be supported. The power claimed never was in use here or acknowledged by the law." From the moment of that decision, slavery ceased to exist in Great Britain, even though two more generations were to pass before it was abolished in Britain's West Indian colonies.[66]

The judicial abolition of slavery in Great Britain gave a firm basis for the growing sentiment against British participation in the slave trade. Led principally by the Quakers, but also including such men as Granville Sharp and William Wilberforce, and backed by such statesmen as Pitt, Burke, and Fox, the Committee for the Abolition of the Slave Trade finally succeeded in having King George III sign,

---

[66]Reginald Coupland, Wilberforce (2d ed.; London, 1945), p. 72. The above passage and some others in the next few pages are taken from Duignan and Clendenen, The United States and the African Slave Trade.

on March 25, 1807, a law under which the slave trade was forbidden to British subjects.[67] The end of the legal slave trade marked a revolution in the relations of Africa with the rest of the world.

Within a few days the United States Congress also enacted a law forbidding the slave trade as of January 1, 1808.[68] The law passed by the United States, however, was largely ineffective, whereas the British law was backed up by the mightiest navy in the world.

Efforts to end the slave trade were to involve the United States in a long series of disputes with Great Britain over American rights at sea, and the United States was also charged with indifference to the horrors of the slave trade. On the other hand, the humanitarian interest of many Americans in ending slavery and the slave trade was closely linked with the establishment of Liberia as a homeland for free American Negroes and as a refuge for Negroes liberated from captured slave ships.

Before the movement to set up a colony in Africa for free Negroes from the United States was given direction and form by the American Colonization Society, strong efforts to arouse sentiment in favor of colonization had been made by a most unusual person, Paul Cuffe. Cuffe, who was half Negro and half Indian, started life in Massachusetts under handicaps imposed both by poverty and by his ancestry. By the time he arrived at early middle age, he had educated himself and had accumulated a substantial fortune as a merchant and shipowner. Being deeply interested in the welfare of the Negro race, he made several voyages to Sierra Leone at his own expense, to see for himself what the colony might offer for the future of the American Negro. In 1816, in cooperation with the African Institution of England and the newly founded American Colonization Society, he transported

---

[67] Coupland, Wilberforce, p. 282.

[68] Both laws became effective on the same date, January 1, 1808.

a number of emigrants from the United States to Sierra Leone, in his own ship and largely with his own funds. Cuffe was a devoted member of the Society of Friends, and his activities reflected the steadfast Quaker attitude toward slavery and the work of rehabilitating Negroes. Thus he helped lay the groundwork on the African coast for the later colonization societies whose efforts were to result in the formation of the Republic of Liberia.[69]

On December 16, 1816, the Reverend Robert Finley, of New Jersey, succeeded in assembling in Washington a group of distinguished citizens for the purpose of organizing a society to promote and assist the colonization in Africa of free Negroes from the United States. The group, which included such men as Henry Clay, Bushrod Washington (nephew of George Washington), John Randolph of Roanoke, and Francis Scott Key, founded the American Colonization Society.[70] The movement thus initiated at Washington spread, slowly at first, but with increasing tempo, until in 1826 there were forty-six auxiliary or local colonization societies. There were state affiliates in every state and territory except Rhode Island, South Carolina, Arkansas, and Michigan.[71]

Within two weeks after the Society was formally organized in Washington, a memorial was submitted to both houses of Congress calling attention to the unfortunate condition of the free Negroes of the United States and urging that they be colonized in Africa. Colonization, the Society stressed in its memorial, would both help the unfortunate

---

[69] Benjamin Brawley, Negro Builders and Heroes (Chapel Hill, N.C., 1937), pp. 35-39; Henry Noble Sherwood, "Paul Cuffe," Journal of Negro History, VIII, No. 2 (1923), 153-229.

[70] Early Lee Fox, The American Colonization Society, 1817-1840 (Baltimore, 1919), p. 46; P.J. Staudenraus, The African Colonization Movement, 1816-1865 (New York, 1961), pp. 27-30.

[71] Fox, The American Colonization Society, p. 61.

Negroes and prevent the greater evils which would be certain to follow if the problem were not solved. A few months later a committee from the Society obtained a personal interview with President Monroe, who proved to be thoroughly sympathetic toward the Society and its aims. Subsequently, the Society appointed two agents to visit Africa to reconnoiter possible sites for a colony.[72]

The two agents, Samuel J. Mills and Ebenezer Burgess, arrived at Sierra Leone in March, 1818. They spent two weeks observing conditions and affairs at the British colony and then started on their detailed examination of the African coast in search of likely sites.[73] For six weeks, in a small sloop manned by Africans, they explored southward from Sierra Leone. Acceptance of the substance of the report submitted by Burgess committed the American Colonization Society to action in the area investigated by the two agents and, at the same time, involved the United States government in African affairs, despite its traditional policies of isolation and noninvolvement.

Within a few months after Burgess' return to the United States, Congress on March 3, 1819, enacted a measure which put some teeth into the law of 1808 forbidding the slave trade. Slavers were declared to be pirates, and the recognized penalty for piracy was death. Of immediate importance to the American Colonization Society was a provision that slaves on board ships captured by the United States Navy should be returned to Africa and liberated. To implement this provision,

---

[72] Ibid., pp. 52-53; Staudenraus, The African Colonization Movement, pp. 37, 41.

[73] They were aided by John Kizell, a former slave in South Carolina. Kizell was one of the Negroes who joined the British in the Revolutionary War; he had been taken to Nova Scotia and from there, finally, to Sierra Leone.

Congress authorized an appropriation of $100,000.[74]

On December 19, 1819, President Monroe, disagreeing with an interpretation of the law by the Attorney General, sent a special message to Congress, stating his personal views and announcing the line of action he intended to take. The President said that the authority he had been given to return captured Africans to Africa implied authority to establish a depot or refuge at some place on the African coast, where the rescued Negroes could be cared for until their final disposition was determined. The Society, meanwhile, had been actively endeavoring to recruit free Negroes who were willing to be the pioneers in the "back to Africa" movement. Eighty-eight such volunteers were assembled, and the Society chartered the 300-ton brig _Elizabeth_ for the voyage to Africa. But there the matter rested, for the Society lacked sufficient funds to proceed further.

At this point President Monroe's personal interest in the Society's aims cleared the way. On January 8, 1820, a month after his message to Congress, he appointed Samuel Bacon the United States agent to supervise the repatriation of rescued slaves, with John B. Bankson as assistant. Bacon was directed by the Secretary of the Navy, acting on behalf of the President, to board and take possession of the _Elizabeth_ and take over her charter, in the name of the United States government. He would then load the vessel with stores and materials necessary to build "barracks" for 300 persons. He would enroll as many artisans as necessary to do the work directed and then immediately sail for the coast of Africa. Upon arrival, he would make arrangements for permission to land and then "make preparations for buildings to shelter the captured Africans and to afford them comfort and protection

---

[74] Robert Earle Anderson, _Liberia, America's African Friend_ (Chapel Hill, N.C., 1952), pp. 64-65.

until they be otherwise disposed of."[75] All this was accomplished by the end of 1820; but the first settlement, at Sherbro Island, was a failure. The survivors were transported to Sierra Leone, where the colonial governor granted them temporary asylum.

In 1821 Dr. Eli Ayres was appointed the Society's new agent. The interest of the government in the enterprise was indicated by the commissioning of Ayres as a naval surgeon and the furnishing of a naval vessel to convey him to Africa. Ayres found the colonists ridden with fever and the agents dead. The survivors were in terror and almost mutinous in their fear. He promptly assumed the duties of both government and Society agent and established necessary discipline with a firm hand. A short time later Navy Lieutenant Robert Stockton arrived with the U.S.S. *Alligator*.

After almost two years the Americans still possessed no land upon which to erect a settlement. Having selected Cape Mesurado as a suitable site, Stockton and Ayres approached the local native potentate, King Peter, to arrange for the purchase, but King Peter refused. After hours of haggling, during which Ayres and Stockton suspected that their lives might be in danger, Stockton dramatically held a loaded pistol to King Peter's head. Next day, the king and five of his principal chiefs formally agreed to the sale. Thus, through the intervention of a United States naval officer and a naval surgeon, the American Colonization Society at last owned a site upon which free Negroes from the United States and rescued Negroes from the slavers could make a new start in life.[76]

---

[75] *Ibid.*, pp. 65-68.

[76] Staudenraus, *The African Colonization Movement*, pp. 63-65. Cape Mesurado is the site of the present city of Monrovia.

The fate of the new colony remained in doubt because of the hostility of the local tribes, who not only resented the loss of their land, but also feared that the new colonists would endanger the slave trade. For generations, tribes on this part of the African coast had been among the most notorious slave sellers. Their fears were undoubtedly played upon by European and American slavers who did not want an end to their lucrative trade.

In 1826 a remarkable white man, Jehudi Ashmun, assumed command of the colony--already called Liberia--and he felt that the colony was now strong enough to take direct and drastic action. Angered by slave raids that had stolen men, women, boys, and girls almost from the doorsteps of Monrovia, the main settlement of the Afro-Americans, Ashmun led a force of twenty-five or thirty men and suddenly swooped down upon a slaving center called Digby. He destroyed a large Spanish-owned barracoon and liberated the slaves. Then, reinforced by officers and men from two American men-of-war that had put in on the coast, he descended upon a notorious slave center known as Trade Town. On arriving, the expedition met a third American warship. The Liberians and Americans landed under fire from the slavers, and the result was the destruction of Trade Town. Few slaves were liberated, but the burning of the town, during which a powder magazine was blown up, and the killing of a considerable number of slavers and their African allies made an impression that was not lost. The slave trade on that part of the coast of Africa never recovered. When Ashmun demanded guarantees from the chiefs that they would abstain from the trade in the future, they had no choice but to yield.

During the period between the initial establishment of the colony and the Liberian declaration of independence in 1847, the position of the United States government was anomalous. Officially, the only interest of the United States in the colony was with its use as a depot for holding slaves rescued by vessels of the United States Navy until their final disposition should be determined. The instructions given to Bacon in 1820 were to the effect that the government had no concern with the affairs of the Colonization Society. Nevertheless, it was the threat of force by a United States naval officer that enabled the colonists to obtain the land they required, and officers and men of the Navy had erected buildings and constructed fortifications after Ashmun's forces defeated the local tribes. The Navy lent aid in Ashmun's expeditions against slavers, and there is little doubt that the American flag flew over the Liberian forces in these affairs.

Although the major efforts at colonization were made by the American Colonization Society,[77] it was not the only one to establish settlements of free Negroes on the African coast. Several of the proliferating state and local colonization societies formulated policies and developed programs independent of, and sometimes in direct competition with, those of the parent society. Consequently, in the decade from 1830 to 1840 a number of settlements were established between Sierra Leone and the Ivory Coast which were unconnected with the older settlements of the American Colonization Society.

Spurred by a disagreement within that Society and fortified by a substantial appropriation from the state legislature, the Maryland Colonization Society was the first to embark upon an independent program. The first agent and group of settlers from Maryland arrived in Africa in 1831 and were somewhat coolly received by the local agent of the American Colonization Society. In 1833, with additional immigrants, the Maryland agent finally obtained a tract of land at Cape Palmas and established "Maryland in Africa." The settlement experienced all the trials, tribulations, and vicissitudes of the older settle-

---

[77]It seems to have been the only organization with which the government dealt directly.

ment, but survived; it finally joined the Republic of Liberia in 1857.[78]

In 1836 the Mississippi Colonization Society decided to establish its own African colony and sent an agent to Africa to obtain land for the purpose. With colonists from Mississippi and Louisiana, a settlement was founded on the Sinoe River. Although started with enthusiasm, the Mississippi-Louisiana settlement failed to prosper. In 1842, the sponsors were easily persuaded to merge their colony with the American Colonization Society.

A third independent effort was made at Bassa Cove in 1834 and 1835 under the joint sponsorship of the New York City organization of the American Colonization Society of Pennsylvania. The pacifistic Quakers were strong in the latter group, and the agent appointed to have charge of the settlement sternly refused to permit any arms and even rejected offers of protection from Monrovia. The tragic result of strict adherence to the belief in pacifism was well illustrated only six months after the colony was established, when the helpless settlers were massacred and the settlement was all but destroyed by hostile tribesmen. Under a new and more realistic governor, the Bassa Cove settlement was re-established, and although relations between it and the older colony were excellent, it was maintained as a separate settlement for several years.[79]

Liberia, from its establishment until the late 1840's, presented a political anomaly. The *de facto* governing bodies were the colonization societies, with the American Colonization Society responsible for the greater part of the settlements, but no society was authorized, by either Act of Congress or any international agreement, to exercise

---

[78] Fox, *The American Colonization Society*, pp. 61-63; A. Doris Banks Henries, *The Liberian Nation: A Short History* (New York, 1954), p. 65.

[79] Henries, *The Liberian Nation*, pp. 67-69.

governmental powers. Nevertheless, a government was necessary, and whether willing or not, the American Colonization Society found itself involved. In 1839, in order to give a semblance of legality to its actions, the Society designated its settlements collectively as the Commonwealth of Liberia and conferred the title of governor upon its agent. Difficulties arose when British traders refused to recognize the authority of the Society's government and British officials in Sierra Leone threatened reprisals against efforts to enforce commercial regulations and collect customs duties. In accordance with tradition, the United States government refused to annex Liberia or assume any official connection. Under the circumstances, the Society took the only feasible course; in 1846 the colony was directed to proclaim its own independence, and in 1847 the Republic of Liberia came into formal being.

This action changed the mission and purpose of the American Colonization Society; it became an emigration society, encouraging and helping free Negroes to migrate to Africa, but it had no responsibility for the operation and management of the colony. No longer burdened with the expenses of governing Liberia, the Society was able to free itself from debt and to devote increasingly large sums toward assisting Negroes who wanted to migrate to Africa. Thus between 1848 and 1854, the Society was able to charter forty-one ships, which carried nearly four thousand persons to Africa. The Civil War, with resulting emancipation and adoption of the 14th Amendment, lessened the attractiveness of Africa to the majority of Negroes, but the activities of the Society continued, on a decreasing scale, until near the end of the century.[80]

---

[80] Staudenraus, The African Colonization Movement, pp. 240-250. The American Colonization Society was still in nominal existence, with six members, as recently as 1959.

Despite the lack of formal recognition, the United States government maintained relations of a sort with the Liberian government, as evidenced by the report of the Secretary of the Interior in 1861, in which it was noted that about 4,500 Africans, rescued from slave ships, had been landed in Liberia in a little more than a year, "under contract made with the Government of Liberia."[81] But the bombardment of Fort Sumter and the exodus of slaveholding Southerners from Washington changed the situation radically. President Lincoln said in his message to Congress on December 3, 1861: "If any good reason exists why we should persevere longer in withholding our recognition of the independence and sovereignty of Hayti and Liberia, I am unable to discern it."[82]

In the press of wartime business, Congress did not act upon the President's recommendation immediately, but in June, 1862, finally gave its approval to recognition of the two Negro republics. Shortly after, an American consul, John Seys, took his post at Monrovia, and the President was able to report in his annual message for 1862 that an advantageous treaty had been concluded with Liberia and was awaiting the Senate's confirmation.[83]

John Seys, the first representative of the United States to be accredited formally to Liberia, is one of those men whose quiet influence has been deeply important but is too often overlooked by historians. A native of the British West Indies and a convert early in

---

[81] Report of the Secretary of the Interior, Senate Executive Documents, 37th Cong., 2d sess., I, 453.

[82] Message of the President, December 3, 1861, Senate Executive Document No. 1, 37th Cong., 2d sess., p. 6.

[83] Message of the President, December 1, 1862, House Executive Document No. 1, 37th Cong., 3d sess., p. 5; letter of the Secretary of State transmitting a report on the commercial relations of the United States, January 6, 1863, House Executive Document No. 28, 37th Cong., 3d sess., p. 1.

life to Methodism, he spent several years in the ministry and in missionary activities in Trinidad and other West Indian islands. Shortly after coming to the United States, he was appointed to a missionary station among the Oneida Indians. His energy, sincerity, and tact gained converts to the point that in a few months he reported he had an interracial church composed of a hundred Indians, seven whites, and one Negro. Meanwhile, the newly established Methodist mission in Liberia was engaging the attention of the church's authorities, and on April 7, 1834, upon the recommendation of Bishop Elijah Hedding, the Board of Managers appointed Seys to that station. He arrived in Liberia on October 18, 1834. Except for a few short visits to the United States, he remained in Liberia until 1841, when he felt compelled to resign owing to difficulties with Governor Thomas Buchanan and to his wife's failing health. The next year, however, on learning that Liberia was without a Methodist missionary, Seys volunteered for service there, in which he continued until 1845, when his wife's ill health again forced him to resign. But he was far from through in Liberia. In 1858 he was appointed United States Government Agent for Freedmen in Liberia and, as just noted, was the first United States Consul.[84]

Early in 1863 the President appointed John J. Henry Commissioner and Consul General to Liberia, but Henry resigned before taking up his post. In his stead, Abraham Hanson formally presented credentials to the President of Liberia on February 25, 1864. Hanson succumbed to an African fever two years later, whereupon the office was tendered to John Seys, who became Minister Resident and Consul

---

[84] Wade Crawford Barclay, History of Methodist Missions, Part I: Early American Methodism, 1769-1844 (New York, 1949-1950), I, 285, 301, 310, 338, 340-343, 344; II, 147.

General in the fall of 1866.[85]

Formal recognition and the designation of diplomatic representatives placed relationships between Liberia and the United States on a regular basis. Before recognition, however, the Liberian government drew moral strength, and sometimes a degree of physical aid, from the friendly interest of the parent country. The presence of the American naval squadron in African waters enabled the struggling Liberian government to act decisively against slavers, and the occasional visit of an American warship was a definite object lesson to African tribes, as in 1852, when the sudden appearance of the U.S.S. John Adams had a very quieting effect upon the chiefs at Grand Bassa. The withdrawal of American ships during the Civil War deprived the Liberian government of this moral and physical aid, and for several years Liberian officials found themselves handicapped in their efforts to extend their authority--and sometimes even to maintain themselves in places they already held.

One of Minister Seys's main interests was the securing of a suitable armed vessel from the United States to enable the Liberian government to suppress slaving and maintain order among the coastal natives. As early as 1864, in his last annual message, President Lincoln had urged that he be given authority to sell to Liberia a gunboat no longer needed by the United States Navy. In 1866 Congress approved such a sale, on terms that would have made the craft practically a gift. Unfortunately, none of the surplus war vessels was suitable--they were either too small for African service or too large for the scanty resources of the Liberian government.

---

[85] Information furnished by Mr. Herman Kahn, Assistant Archivist for Civil Archives, National Archives, Washington, D.C., in a letter to the authors, July 11, 1962. It is not clear why the first representatives to Liberia (and Haiti as well) were designated commissioners, instead of ministers. Seys was the first to hold the title of Minister.

The basis for the American Colonization Society's activities in Liberia was the widely held idea that the Negro of the Western Hemisphere should better his lot by migrating to the ancestral homeland, Africa. "Back to Africa" schemes enjoyed a degree of popularity, especially among a number of educated free Negroes who were discouraged by the handicaps imposed upon Negroes in a predominantly Caucasian society.[86] Such a person was Martin Robison Delany. He was born in 1812 of free Negro parents, in the region which is now West Virginia. Supposedly he was a descendant of Mandinka royalty of the Niger Valley. After a boyhood troubled by racial discrimination, he engaged in journalism and studied medicine. Upon receiving a medical degree from Harvard College in 1852, he established a practice at Chatham, Ontario. But even in Canada he felt the force of racial prejudice and discrimination.

While still a medical student, Delany aspired to be a medical missionary to Africa. He seems to have dropped the idea for several years, although he never lost sight of the unhappy condition of his race in America. In 1854 he was a member and leading spirit of a convention called to consider a scheme of emigration from the United States to some other parts of the Western Hemisphere--Africa was specifically excluded from consideration. The convention adopted appropriate resolutions and established a National Board of Commissioners to endeavor to implement the resolutions.

Delany had, however, been maturing a scheme to organize and finance an exploration of the Niger Valley with a view to settlement there. His plan was to obtain a cargo of trade goods in Philadelphia and exchange these for beeswax and ivory at Loango. With the profits from these transactions, he would go to Lagos and thence to the Yoruba

---

[86] See L.R. Mehlinger, "The Attitude of the Free Negro toward African Colonization," Journal of Negro History, I (1916), 276-301.

country of Nigeria. The Board approved this proposal and on August 30, 1858, published an announcement:

> The object of this Expedition is to make a Topographical, Geological and Geographical Examination of the Valley of the River Niger, in Africa, and an inquiry into the state and condition of the people of that valley, and other parts of Africa, together with such other scientific inquiries as may by them be deemed expedient, for the purposes of science and for general information; and without any reference to, and with the Board being entirely opposed to any Emigration there as such. Provided, however, that nothing in this Instrument be so construed as to interfere with the right of the Commissioners to negotiate on their own behalf, or that of any other parties, or organization for territory.[87]

The dichotomy in the announced objectives was unhappily reflected in the selection of personnel for the expedition. From the start, Delany's activities lacked coordination with those of some of his subordinates. When Delany's sailing was delayed until May, 1859, his assistant, Robert Campbell, a Jamaica-born chemist, departed for England and upon his own initiative persuaded several wealthy Englishmen to provide financial support for the project. Campbell stressed the desirability of finding a supply of cotton for the mills of Manchester and prevailed upon Lord Malmesbury, Secretary of State for Foreign Affairs, to give him a letter of introduction to various officials in Africa. Arriving at Lagos on July 21, 1859, Campbell, without waiting for Delany, moved upcountry to Abeokuta in August, accompanied by the sons of Samuel Crowther, a famous and highly esteemed native Nigerian missionary.

Delany arrived later, without introduction, but managed to get to the court of the king of the Egba tribe and on December 27, 1859, obtained a treaty. In return for pledges that none but people of good

---

[87] Quoted in A.H.M. Kirk-Greene, "America in the Niger Valley: A Colonization Centenary," Phylon, XXIII (1962), 230-231.

character would come to Africa, immigrants of the Negro race were granted the privilege of settling in Egba territory, where they would be subject to Egba law and custom. They were to bring with them "Intelligence, Education, a Knowledge of the Arts and Sciences, Agriculture, and other Mechanical and Industrial Occupations."[88] The treaty was later repudiated by the Alake (king), allegedly because of pressure from British missionaries. It is interesting to note that Delany and Campbell found one American Negro already settled in the region they proposed to colonize.[89]

Delany and Campbell returned first to England and then to the United States to raise the necessary funds and assemble emigrants. They were supported by numerous influential persons and by organizations such as the African Aid Society, of London. There was nothing inherently impracticable in Delany's plan for the colonization of American Negroes in the Niger Valley; certainly the difficulties would have been no more formidable than those encountered in Liberia and Sierra Leone. But soon, in the turmoil of the American Civil War, the status of the American Negro was to be redefined and all schemes for African colonization were to be suspended. Delany went into the war effort, heart and soul, finally being commissioned in the Medical Corps of the army. After the war he served as a federal official in South Carolina--one of the few "carpet-bag" officials who earned the praise of the Carolinians for his honesty and efficiency in office.

Although the plan for resettlement of American Negroes in Nigeria was never put into effect, the explorations made by Delany and Campbell were not without value. Both of these observers made

---

[88] _Ibid._, p. 235.

[89] Robert Campbell, _A Pilgrimage to My Motherland: An Account of a Journey among the Egbas and Yorubas of Central Africa, in 1859-60_ (New York, 1861), pp. 109-110.

definite contributions to the world's knowledge of African life.[90]

The Missionary Movement

Closely related to the various colonization movements, and to some extent growing out of them, was a widespread desire to bring Christianity to the heathen of the Dark Continent. Religious interest in Africa by Americans was not new. A short time after the Revolutionary War, a former slave known as Olaudah Equiano, or Gustavus Vassa, who had been owned in Virginia and probably converted to Christianity there, petitioned the Bishop of London for ordination, with the intention of going to Africa as a missionary. The bishop refused--the world was not yet ready to attempt to evangelize Africa--but the seed had been planted and was ready to germinate.[91] Even earlier, five years before the outbreak of the Revolutionary War, Samuel Hopkins of Newport, Rhode Island, proposed to train a number of carefully chosen free Negroes for the ministry and send them to Guinea. There they were to settle quietly and watch for favorable opportunities to teach Africans the doctrines and precepts of Christianity. Each was to constitute himself a focus for Christian effort and teaching. The war prevented Hopkins from putting his plan into effect immediately, but after the war he selected a number of candidates and began training them. Hopkins died in 1803, before the education of any of his missionaries had been completed, but at least two of his men, identified as S.

---

[90] For a scholarly discussion of Delany and his projects see Kirk-Greene, "America in the Niger Valley," pp. 225-239. Other sources are M.R. Delany, Official Report of the Niger Valley Exploring Party (New York, 1861); F.A. Rollin, Life and Public Services of Martin R. Delany (Boston, 1868); Robert Campbell, A Few Facts Relating to Lagos, Abeokuta, and Other Sections of Central Africa (Philadelphia, 1860) and A Pilgrimage to My Motherland.

[91] The Interesting Narrative of the Life of Olaudah Equiano, or Gustavus Vassa, the African, Written by Himself (London, 1789), pp. 3-25, cited in Thomas L. Hodgkin, Nigerian Perspectives (London, 1960), p. 155.

Nubia and N. Gardner, went to Africa later, under the auspices of the American Colonization Society.[92]

The first American religious impression upon Africa seems to have been made at Sierra Leone, the earliest of the colonies established for repatriating freed Africans in their ancestral continent. An important element among the colonists, possibly a majority, was formed by the Nova Scotians--slaves who had fought with the British forces during the Revolutionary War. Most of the Nova Scotians were deeply religious, giving their loyalties to the Baptist, Wesleyan, or Huntingdonian churches. The first arrivals from America included entire congregations led by their pastors; among the ministers, who were also captains, were Cato Perkins and William Ash, natives of Charleston, South Carolina. Churches were among the first structures erected in the new colony.[93]

It was not long before the Church Missionary Society of London and other religious bodies sent missionaries to Sierra Leone to keep the colonists within paths of denominational orthodoxy and to begin work among the pagan natives.[94] Probably the first American to serve as a missionary in Africa was the Negro (his name is not recorded)

---

[92]Wilber Christian Harr, "The Negro as an American Protestant Missionary in Africa" (unpublished Ph.D. dissertation, University of Chicago Divinity School, 1945), pp. 12-13; William D. Johnston, "Slavery in Rhode Island, 1755-1776," Publications of the Rhode Island Historical Society, II (1894), 154-155.

[93]Christopher Fyfe, "The West African Methodists in the Nineteenth Century," Sierra Leone Bulletin of Religion, III, No. 1 (1961), 22-23, and "The Countess of Huntingdon's Connexion in Nineteenth Century Sierra Leone," ibid., IV, No. 2 (1962), 53-54; see also Fyfe's History of Sierra Leone, p. 38.

[94]Fyfe, "The Countess of Huntingdon's Connexion," pp. 54-55, credits Cato Perkins with having inspired one of the founders of the London Missionary Society to think of missions in Africa.

who was added to the staff of the Sierra Leone mission of the Church Missionary Society in 1814 because of his knowledge of several African languages.[95]

The first missionaries to go directly from the United States to Africa were Negroes, and their efforts were directed toward Liberia. It was assumed by most churches that a Negro could work among the heathen natives of Africa more readily than could a white man. It was assumed, too, that devout Christian free Negroes were anxious to return to their ancestral homeland. Furthermore, the African coast was "the white man's grave," so that the odds were against any white missionary's surviving long enough to accomplish any good. Negroes were sent in the hope and belief that they were immune to the deadly fevers of Africa.

None of these assumptions were true. Immunity to disease proved to be an individual matter, rather than a racial characteristic, and the death toll among the American Negro missionaries was as frightful as among the white men. To the native African the American Negro was not a compatriot, but instead was another foreigner--and a foreigner who had much more in common with the white men than he did with any African. Cultural ties between the American and African Negroes were practically nonexistent. Nevertheless, the American Negro as a missionary in Africa has played an important role.

It is true that at certain times and among a few denominations there was a degree of opposition to the Negro as a missionary, but nevertheless, during the nineteenth century, many Negroes were sent to Africa as missionaries by white missionary groups. Hence, such a statement as that recently made by Harold Isaacs is certainly

---

[95] Charles Pelham Groves, The Planting of Christianity in Africa (London, 1948-1958), I, 216.

open to question: "With but rare exceptions, the large white Christian denominations seldom wished to send Negro workers into the African vineyards. Even when they did wish it, they seldom did so, and when they did, they did it sparingly and not for long."[96] On the contrary, the evidence indicates that most of the Christian bodies supporting African missions were anxious to send Negro missionaries and were limited only by the availability of suitably qualified Negroes. A very high proportion of the missionaries sent to Liberia were Negroes. Nearly every missionary pioneer was accompanied by Negro assistants. Thomas J. Bowen, of the Southern Baptist Church, for example, establishing missions for his church in Nigeria in 1849, was accompanied by Negro missionaries. William H. Sheppard, a Negro missionary, set up the earliest Presbyterian missions in the Congo and remained in that field for many years, with both white and Negro missionaries to assist him. The Reverend Charles W. Thomas, cruising the African coast as a navy chaplain in the 1850's, found Negro missionaries wherever Christian missions existed.[97]

In 1821, the first shipload of colonists from America to the region that was to become Liberia included among its passengers the Reverend Daniel Coker, from Baltimore. He was a former slave who

---

[96] Harold R. Isaacs, The New World of Negro Americans (New York, 1963), p. 124.

[97] Harr, "The Negro as an American Protestant Missionary in Africa," pp. 20, 50-53; see also Thomas, Adventures and Observations on the West Coast of Africa and Its Islands, pp. 99-100; William H. Sheppard, Presbyterian Pioneers in Congo (Richmond, Va., n.d.), passim. When the Ethiopian and Zionist churches sprang up after 1900, the colonial powers sought to discourage Negro missionaries. The fears engendered by Chilembwe in Nyasaland, Kitawala in the Congo, and the Watch Tower movement in Northern Rhodesia made it difficult for American Negro missionaries to gain entrance into colonial territories, but white Christian churches cannot be blamed for this.

had managed to purchase his own freedom and obtain a liberal education and was a member and minister of the African Methodist Episcopal Church from its origin as a national organization in 1816. During the voyage to Africa, he organized a congregation, and when, after landing, the three agents of the Colonization Society died, the leadership of the colony fell upon him. It was he who led the decimated remains of the first colony to Sierra Leone for refuge. He remained in Sierra Leone after the Americans returned to the re-established colony and for many years was the highly respected pastor of the African Methodists of the British colony.[98]

Among the first colonists in Liberia were Lott Carey (or Cary) and Colin Teague, two Negro ministers from the Baptist Board of Foreign Missions. Little has been recorded about Teague, but of Lott Carey, fortunately, more is known. He was born a slave in Virginia about 1780. With help from a minister, he taught himself to read and write. He was rented to the owners of a warehouse and soon made himself so valuable that they paid him a regular wage in addition to the rent paid his master. Thus he was able to purchase freedom for himself and his children. In 1819, being accepted by the American Colonization Society as a missionary and ordained by the Baptist General Convention, Carey sailed for Liberia; there he remained for the rest of his life.[99]

---

[98] Barclay, Early American Methodism, I, 327-328; Fyfe, A History of Sierra Leone, pp. 132-133, 181, 257.

[99] Information on Carey is found in Miles Mark Fisher, "Lott Cary, the Colonizing Missionary," Journal of Negro History, VII (1922), 380-418; Edward A. Freeman, The Epoch of Negro Baptists and the Foreign Mission Board (Kansas City, Kans., 1953), pp. 107-109; William Gammell, A History of American Baptist Missions in Asia, Africa, Europe, and North America, under the Care of the American Baptist Missionary Union (Boston, 1854), pp. 244-248; Harr, "The Negro as an American Protestant Missionary in Africa," pp. 46-47.

Negro Baptists later sent their own missionaries to Africa, and a Lott Carey Missionary Society was established in 1897. (Information supplied by Dr. St Clair Drake, Roosevelt University.)

Within a few years the other principal Protestant denominations in the United States sent missionaries to Liberia to work among the repatriated settlers. They met with varying degrees of success, but without exception all suffered from the climate and deadly fevers. One after another, often within a few days or weeks after their arrival in Africa, the earnest, hopeful young Americans succumbed. The first Methodist missionary, Melville B. Cox, died four months after reaching Liberia.[100] On New Year's Day, 1834, a second group of Methodists arrived--five men and women, of whom two died within three months. Two of those remaining lost heart and returned to America, but a lone courageous woman, Sophronia Farrington, stuck to her post, and through her efforts and example the Methodist mission survived.[101] The Reverend John Pinney, who arrived in Liberia in 1833 as the first missionary ever dispatched by the Presbyterian Church in the United States to a foreign field, similarly survived. One assistant after another succumbed to African fevers with heartbreaking regularity, but Pinney retained his health and determination. In addition to preaching the Gospel, for some time he acted as agent of the American Colonization Society and was in charge of the colony. Thus he is justly numbered among the founders and fathers of Liberia. Not until 1839 did he retire from the mission field and finally return to America.[102]

The missionaries mentioned thus far were concerned primarily with the spiritual welfare of the Negro colonists from the United States. Although they all considered their work among the Liberians a preparation for the later conversion of the seemingly countless hordes of

---

[100] Cox died uttering the famous words, "Though a thousand fall, let not Africa be given up." See Johannes Du Plessis, The Evangelisation of Pagan Africa (Cape Town, 1930), p. 100.

[101] Groves, The Planting of Christianity in Africa, I, 296.

[102] Ibid., pp. 296-297.

heathen who surrounded the colony, none of them came equipped or prepared for that further labor. A few years before the events just mentioned, however, the American Board of Commissioners for Foreign Missions had been formed on an interdenominational basis for just such work. In 1825 the Board adopted a resolution looking to the establishment of a mission in West Africa as soon as this would be practicable and shortly thereafter appointed a Negro Presbyterian minister to work among the natives of Liberia. For some unspecified reason, the minister was not sent, and the project remained in abeyance until 1833, when "the Committee were constrained, by their views of the imperative claims of Africa, to resume the subject."[103] Later in the same year, the Reverend John Leighton Wilson volunteered his services and on November 28 departed for Africa, accompanied by Stephen R. Wyncoop as his assistant.

Wilson was instructed to determine the suitability of Cape Palmas as a location for a mission, and if he found no serious objections or obstacles, he would "take measures for the speedy commencement of a mission there." He would then devote himself to acquiring all possible information about Liberia and the native tribes, with a new departure in missionary work as his final objective--the training of natives for the evangelization of their fellow Africans:

> The information you will...seek concerning the native tribes, will relate to the character of their superstitions; the hold these have on the minds of the people; the nature of their vices; their social condition; their various languages; how far the gospel may be preached to them; their disposition in respect to schools;...the probability of

---

[103] Missionary Herald, XXIX (1833), 19. For the sake of convenience, the American Board of Commissioners for Foreign Missions will hereafter be referred to as "the American Board," or simply as "the Board," except where the lengthier expression is more appropriate. The "Committee" referred to above was the Prudential Committee, which was the Board's governing body.

> procuring helpers from among the sons of Africa, or of the colonists; and the expediency of sending them from among the colored people of this country.[104]

The important feature of the Board's instructions lay in the fact that Wilson was to train Africans, rather than endeavor to carry on the work of evangelization by his own efforts or by the efforts of Americans only: "The main dependence of our mission in western Africa...must be upon the labors of pious natives and colonists, trained for the work in seminaries provided for the purpose, and acting under the superintendence of missionaries sent from this country." Wilson's major personal objective was the formulation of an educational and training program to enable Africans to evangelize and convert their own people.[105]

Wilson and his assistant, Wyncoop, arrived at the Liberian coast in the latter part of January, 1834. They spent the next several weeks between Cape Mount and Cape Palmas, exploring, observing, and asking questions, and decided that Cape Palmas, where the Maryland Colony had recently been established, was the most suitable location. They returned to the United States to report their findings to the Board, arriving at New York on April 13, 1834. The Board quickly approved their recommendations, and on November 7, a little less than a year after his first embarkation, Wilson, with his wife and a Negro woman teacher as assistant, sailed again for Africa. By August, 1835, Wilson was able to report to the Board from Cape Palmas that a small

---

[104] Ibid., p. 401.

[105] Ibid. In addition, it was the Board's hope that its missions would ultimately extend from the base that Wilson would establish to the depths of the unknown Niger Valley and the slopes of the "Mountains of the Moon": "An object of primary importance in respect to the inland parts of western Africa, and the central portions of the continent eastward of the Niger, is *the exploration of the country with a view to missionary operations*" (p. 402; italics in original).

school had been opened, with both natives and the children of colonists as pupils. Mrs. Wilson was conducting two Sabbath schools, one for Africans, the other for Americans. Wilson himself was exploring the surrounding country, studying the people, learning their customs and beliefs, and endeavoring to gain their confidence.[106]

During the next few years several other missionaries from the United States as well as a number of teachers and craftsmen followed Wilson to Cape Palmas. The Grebo language was reduced to writing, and textbooks, tracts, parts of the Bible, and a life of Christ were translated for use in the schools and in teaching Africans the principles of the Christian faith. A Negro printer arrived from the United States with a press, which was soon in operation printing books, pamphlets, and tracts, not only for the Board's mission but for other missions as well.[107] The mission at Cape Palmas, under Wilson's leadership, appeared to be fairly on the way to becoming a center of Christian activities in West Africa.

But the missionaries of the American Board, as well as those of other churches and nationalities, often found themselves struggling, sometimes unsuccessfully, against all sorts of difficulties. There was always the danger of the dreaded and deadly "African fever"; the country was unsettled and frequently turbulent; and there were annoying administrative troubles with the colonization societies. The Amero-Liberians were lukewarm in their attitude toward Christianizing and civilizing the aborigines, and there was a marked indifference, and sometimes downright hostility, among the Africans--this in spite of

---

[106] Ibid., XXX (1834), 212-219; XXXII (1836), 4, 64-66, 409-414.

[107] Ibid., XXXVII (1841), 138-139. Wilson informed the Board in September, 1840, that he was printing a Bassa spelling book and a hymnbook for the Baptist mission at Bassa. Since the Baptists were "very much straitened from want of funds," this work was being done gratis.

the happy optimism of nearly all missionary reports. Even natives who welcomed, or accepted, the missionaries often saw no reason to extend the benefits of the missionaries to neighboring communities and tribes. In 1836, for example, Wilson reported to the Board that the natives at Cape Palmas were decidedly antagonistic to his proposed establishment of a mission among their traditional enemies at Rocktown, only a short distance away.[108]

The worst enemy, however, was disease. The medical and sanitary knowledge of the time was insufficient to solve the problem. West Africa continued to live up to its ancient reputation as "the white man's grave," and there was soon abundant evidence that it was as fatal to the American Negro as to the Caucasian. In 1834 the American Colonization Society learned that of 649 colonists dispatched to Liberia in the few months preceding, 134 had died already. The Church Missionary Society of London recorded that 89 missionaries were sent to West Africa between 1804 and 1825 and that 54 had died there.[109]

Wilson and his wife enjoyed several months of apparent immunity, but eventually the fever struck them too, and for months they were on the threshold of death. Finally they recovered, and the fact that they did not succumb, either to the initial attacks of the fever or in any of the subsequent periods of relapse, makes them outstanding in the missionary annals of West Africa. Still other of the eager souls who arrived hopefully to assist in promoting the Kingdom of God were not so fortunate. The Reverend David White and his wife arrived at Cape Palmas on Christmas Day, 1836; less than a month later he was dead,

---

[108] Ibid., XXXII (1836), 413. See also Du Plessis, The Evangelisation of Pagan Africa, pp. 100-102.

[109] Missionary Herald, XXX (1834), 187; Philip D. Curtin, The Image of Africa: British Ideas and Action, 1780-1850 (Madison, Wis., 1964), p. 484.

and his wife, who had also been taken ill, lived only a few days longer. At almost the same time an American Negro teacher named Polk, whom Wilson had praised highly in several reports, was fatally stricken. In 1841 the first medical missionary, Dr. Alexander Wilson, died suddenly, and in 1842 the wife of the Reverend William Walker died after seeming to be on the way to recovery.[110]

Many people will take a chance on possible martyrdom, but there are very few who would willingly face almost certain death. That it became increasingly difficult to obtain missionaries for West Africa is not surprising, especially when the evangelical fervor of the 1820's and 1830's began to decline. Hence, in the early 1840's, the American Board decided to transfer its activities to some other region of West Africa. The Missionary Herald noted in January, 1843, that Wilson and Benjamin Griswold had gone "eastward" in the preceding May to search for a suitable location. They decided upon a site near the mouth of the Gabon River, where the Africans received them cordially and the climate and surroundings seemed to be more healthful than at Cape Palmas. The Gabon was, moreover, a trading center, visited by English, French, and American vessels, so that regular communication with civilization was possible. The people, too, one of the missionaries reported, were "a good deal more advanced in civilization than any natives I have before seen or expected to see on the western coast of Africa." For these reasons, the Gabon seemed to be the best location for a mission.[111]

The Board's mission and activities at Cape Palmas were turned over to missionaries of the Protestant Episcopal Church, who had been working in the Maryland Colonization Society's settlements since 1836.

---

[110] Missionary Herald, XXXIII (1837), 219-220, 269, 364-367; XXXVIII (1842), 172, 177-179, 412-413.

[111] Ibid., XXXVIII (1842), 381, 497-500.

Except for this mission, Protestant missions in Liberia were virtually abandoned during the period between the proclamation of Liberia's independence and the Civil War in the United States. The toll of missionary lives was too heavy to be sustained. Nevertheless, the Episcopalians hung on doggedly, although in three years' time, out of twenty-two missionaries, ten died and eight were invalided home. There were times when the missionaries were endangered by native uprisings; on two or three occasions they had to close the mission temporarily. They also faced the shortsighted opposition of the Liberian citizens to missionary work among the indigenous people. But in spite of such discouragements the Christianizing and educational work initiated by Wilson was continued without significant interruption for many years.[112] The survival of the Episcopal mission was largely due to the determination of Bishop John Payne. He was born in Westmoreland County, Virginia, and educated at the College of William and Mary and the Alexandria Theological Seminary. He went to Liberia as a young man and spent the greater part of his life there; in 1853 he was consecrated as bishop. He was instrumental in bringing the Reverend Alexander Crummell to Liberia and starting him on his lifework.[113]

During the early part of 1843 the American Board missionaries transferred themselves and their belongings from Cape Palmas to the Gabon. As at Cape Palmas, they started to work almost as soon as they landed. Just when they felt that they were beginning to make progress, the very existence of the mission was threatened by a new factor

---

[112] Du Plessis, The Evangelisation of Pagan Africa, pp. 103-104. See also the Thomas Jefferson Bowen Papers, MSS held by the Southern Baptist Convention Historical Commission, Nashville.

[113] See "Biographical Index," Calendar of the Manuscripts in the Schomburg Collection of Negro Literature (microfilmed typescript [Ann Arbor and London, University Microfilms]); Appleton's Cyclopedia of American Biography (New York, 1888-1889), IV, 685.

in African affairs--the imperial ambitions of Europe. Benjamin Griswold informed the Board in a letter written on May 8, 1843, that a French naval officer, with a small squadron, had attempted to purchase land for a fort on the south bank of the river and that later officers from two French men-of-war had made a similar attempt on the north shore. He believed that they had been successful in making the purchase. Griswold, as a devoted evangelical, feared that this might give an entry to the "Romanists," but apparently saw no other danger.[114]

A year later, in April, 1844, Walker informed the Board that scarcely a week had passed without efforts by the French to persuade the natives to place themselves under French protection and that finally, by pure chicanery, these efforts had succeeded. King Glass, the local chief, he said, had, while very drunk, signed a paper which was supposed to be a letter of friendship to King Louis Philippe, but was actually a treaty in which he submitted to French overlordship. The next day the commander of a French warship exhibited the paper to King Glass and received his acknowledgment that he had signed it. Thus the treaty was signed and "ratified."[115] In the ensuing difficulties, the American missionaries found themselves in a dangerous position. After several futile attempts to persuade the natives to accept the treaty and admit French sovereignty, the French realized that they would have to use force. They hunted for an excuse to consider themselves insulted. A French officer brusquely informed the missionaries that he could not guarantee their safety if he had to bombard the town--and added curtly that they had no official status whatsoever. Since the Africans still refused to hoist the French flag, the bombardment started. A thirty-two-pound shot smashed into the mission church;

---

[114] Missionary Herald, XXXIX (1843), 404.

[115] Ibid., XL (1844), 349-351.

the missionaries had displayed an American flag, but to no avail. A French landing party fired indiscriminately at all natives, further endangering the Americans and their property.[116]

A few weeks later, Wilson informed the Board that the local French commander had hinted broadly that he would be glad to have the Americans leave Gabon, a hint to which Wilson had replied spiritedly that he would not leave until he had received a formal, written command to do so. Three months later, the mission's boats and other property which the French had seized at the beginning of the trouble had not been returned, and Wilson fully expected to be expelled as soon as the anticipated French Jesuits arrived. By January, 1846, however, the situation began to appear more hopeful. A representative of the French admiral came to the mission, apologized in the admiral's name for the dangers to which the mission had been exposed, and assured Wilson of the admiral's friendship. Quietly, the mission continued to carry on its educational and religious program with what Wilson considered a promising degree of success. Nevertheless, he recommended to the Board that locations outside the French sphere should be selected, to which the mission could be transferred quickly, if necessary.[117]

During the height of the trouble the missionaries were unable to appeal to their own government. Distances made appeal impossible, and no American ship of war was on that part of the coast. Meanwhile, the local French authorities were reluctant to permit a newly arrived missionary and his wife to land; a temporary permit was somewhat grudgingly granted, after a delay and some argument. But the situation changed completely when Commodore George C. Read, commander of the American squadron, arrived at Gabon in mid-1846. He wrote a letter--apparently a strong letter--to the French admiral who com-

---

[116] Ibid., XLII (1846), 25-31. The bombardment occurred in July, 1845.

[117] Ibid., pp. 104, 157-158, 210-211, 316.

manded all French forces on the coast. Soon afterward, the admiral made a personal visit to the mission, and Wilson reported to the Board: "Since the visit of the French admiral and Commodore Read, both of whom showed us much kindness, we have experienced nothing but the most civil treatment, both from the local authorities, and such of the officers of the French navy as have occasionally visited the river."[118]

With that, the worst of the difficulties of the Board's mission in West Africa were over; it was not long before the French authorities recognized that the American missionaries were a positive force for good. From then until the mission was turned over to the Presbyterians, some thirty years later, the Americans enjoyed extremely favorable relations with both the French overlords and their African subjects.[119]

As in all other regions, the first efforts of the missionaries at Gabon were devoted to studying the languages of the natives and translating religious material into idioms that could be understood. Because of the uncertainty and vicissitudes of the first years at Gabon, the printing press (brought from Cape Palmas) was not set up and put into operation until 1849. Wilson himself had to act as printer. Meanwhile, Walker had translated the Gospel of St. Matthew into the Mpongwe language; this was probably the first book published at Gabon.[120] By the time the mission was turned over to the Presbyterians, both the Mpongwe and the Bakele languages had been reduced to writing and their grammatical principles worked out; vocabularies had been compiled and

---

[118] Ibid., XLIII (1847), 257.

[119] Groves, The Planting of Christianity in Africa, II, 67-70; Missionary Herald, XLVIII (1852), 58; Clifton Jackson Phillips, "Protestant America and the Pagan World: The First Half Century of the American Board of Commissioners for Foreign Missions" (unpublished Ph.D. dissertation, Harvard University, 1954), p. 223.

[120] Missionary Herald, XLVI (1850), 38.

extensive passages from the Gospels translated and printed.[121]

For years after the first establishment of missions on the West Coast of Africa, the vast region that is now called Nigeria remained untouched. The Niger River Valley itself was still largely unknown.[122] Nevertheless, disturbed by the probability that recovered slaves, repatriated from Sierra Leone, would revert to paganism, the British Wesleyans and the Church Missionary Society of the Church of England made a beginning in Nigeria in the early 1840's. In 1846, after having spent almost two years on the coast while vainly trying to get to the interior, Henry Townsend and Samuel A. Crowther established the first Christian mission at Abeokuta, the capital of the Yoruba tribe.[123]

Meanwhile, in the United States, the Southern Baptists were giving anxious consideration to an African mission. In 1849 the Reverend Thomas Jefferson Bowen arrived in Nigeria to explore for a suitable location. In background and early life Bowen was almost unique among missionaries. A native of Georgia, he had raised and commanded a company of Georgia volunteers in the war against the Creek Indians in 1836. Later in the same year, with his taste for adventure and excitement still unsatisfied, he went to the Southwest and enlisted in the army of the infant Republic of Texas. He was immediately commissioned a captain of cavalry in that redoubtable force and spent the next two years on the Far Western frontier, fighting Indians and bandits. In 1840, after

---

[121] Du Plessis, The Evangelisation of Pagan Africa, p. 174.

[122] This was true despite two carefully organized exploring expeditions, in 1832 and 1842, both of which ended in disaster.

[123] Du Plessis, The Evangelisation of Pagan Africa, pp. 134-137. Samuel Adjai Crowther was a native African rescued from slavery by the Royal Navy and converted to Christianity at Sierra Leone. He was an apt scholar. Crowther was a member of the disastrous exploring expedition of 1842, and shortly afterward he was ordained by the Bishop of London. He was later the first Anglican Bishop of Nigeria and the first African to hold such an ecclesiastical office.

leaving the Texas service and returning to Georgia, he underwent a deep emotional experience and devoted the remainder of his life to preaching.[124]

In Nigeria, Bowen established friendly relations with the Church of England missionaries. They gave him every assistance and encouragement, and he was deeply impressed by them and their efforts.[125] Anxious not to duplicate their work or to interfere with missions already established, Bowen set off to explore Nigeria and spent the next two years searching for a suitable site. Usually alone, except for a few bearers, he ran into all sorts of difficulties. Some Nigerian chiefs were friendly; more were suspicious or even hostile. The witch doctors by this time suspected that missionary influence meant the end of their own, and the numerous Moslems used every means to prevent his penetration into their areas. Nevertheless, by a combination of sincerity, earnestness, and humor, as well as an impressive skill with firearms, he won his way and visited parts of the Niger Valley that no white man had ever seen before. In every sense of the term, Bowen was an explorer, although he did not regard himself as such.[126]

Bowen found himself in Nigeria at a most critical time. There was civil war within Yorubaland, and the slave-raiding Dahomeans chose the early 1850's to attack. The Dahomeans were finally repulsed and defeated, but not until they had attacked the Egba capital of Abeokuta,

---

[124] E.C. Routh, "Thomas Jefferson Bowen," The Encyclopedia of Southern Baptists (Nashville, 1958), I, 183.

[125] In a letter written to a friend, dated at Iketu, May 16, 1851, he said: "Some of these Episcopalians were laboring in Africa when I was a wicked young man in the Texas cavalry, ranging the prairies of the western frontier with my sword and yager." Bowen Papers.

[126] Thcmas Jefferson Bowen, Central Africa: Adventures and Missionary Labors in Several Countries in the Interior of Africa, from 1849 to 1856 (Charleston, 1857), passim.

where Bowen had taken refuge with his Church of England friends. It was largely through the leadership and example of the missionaries that the Egba people were able to defeat their enemies in battle at Aro in 1851.[127]

Bowen returned to the United States in 1852, married, and was again in Nigeria the following year, this time as the head of a small group of Southern Baptist missionaries. They established themselves at Ogbonoshaw (Ogbomosho), north of Abeokuta, in the heart of the Egba country. In spite of the usual deaths and many difficulties, the mission survived. Bowen and his wife returned to the United States in 1856; his health was shattered, although he was destined to live for many years longer.

Bowen's significance in the story of American relations with Africa and interest in the continent is large. As an explorer and a linguist, he deserves to be known as one of the foremost. His researches in the Yoruba language were among the first scholarly studies of that idiom, and his Yoruba grammar and dictionary was the standard work for a long time; his accounts of the interior of Nigeria gave the Western world a far more accurate description of that mysterious region and its people than had existed before.[128] As a sincere friend of the people of Nigeria, he was a bitter enemy of the slave trade, and his name appears, along with those of the Church of England missionaries, as a

---

[127]Bowen makes no mention of this episode in any of his surviving letters, but Biobaku says that the Texas cavalryman virtually directed the defense of the walls. S.O. Biobaku, The Egba and Their Neighbours, 1842-1872 (Oxford, 1957), p. 44. See also Michael Crowder, The Story of Nigeria (London, 1962), pp. 126-130.

[128]See T.J. Bowen, Grammar and Dictionary of the Yoruba Language, with an Introductory Description of the Country and People of Yoruba (Washington, 1858), and Meroke; or, Missionary Life in Africa (Philadelphia, 1858). The latter work is anonymous, but was revised by Bowen. It is a biographical sketch of Henry Townsend, one of the Church of England missionaries whom Bowen particularly admired.

witness to the Treaty of Abeokuta (1852) by which the local king pledged himself to abolish the traffic.[129] He tried, in 1857, to get Congress to negotiate a trade treaty with the Yoruba and to support an exploration of the Niger River, and was interested in promoting "back to Africa" schemes.[130]

Thus far, no mention has been made of the missionary efforts of the American Roman Catholics in West Africa. The American missionary movement of the early nineteenth century was largely a Protestant movement; the Catholic Church in the United States was still establishing itself. Nevertheless, American Catholicism was represented in West Africa from an early date, and Catholics from the United States were among the pioneers of their faith in the field.

In 1833, the Bishop of Charleston, South Carolina, suggested the advisability of sending Catholic missionaries to Liberia, especially since the settlements of the Maryland Colonization Society at Cape Palmas presumably included a number of Catholics. Some time later, Pope Gregory XVI asked the bishops of New York and Philadelphia each

---

[129] Bowen Papers.

[130] See Bowen Papers, letter, October 10, 1859, to the Reverend A.M. Pointdexter, in which Bowen speaks of his visit to New York City to promote "emigration among the Blacks." It is possible that there was some connection between Bowen's scheme and Martin Robison Delany's Niger Valley exploration of 1859. This is purely conjectural, however, and is based entirely upon the coincidence of dates.

In 1858 Bowen attempted to found a Southern Baptist mission in Brazil, but was unsuccessful. He served briefly as a chaplain in the Confederate Army in the Civil War and spent most of the remainder of his life preaching and endeavoring to regain his shattered health. His intense suffering caused periods of near insanity, but he was always sustained by his fervent religious faith. He never lost his interest in Africa or the hope someday to return. In 1859, when the church was considering the abandonment of the Nigeria mission because of the mortality among the missionaries, he wrote to Pointdexter: "Shall we abandon sixty millions of people to heathenism, and to eternal perdition, because they live in a sickly climate?"

to designate a priest; in response, Monsignor Edward W. Barron, the Vicar-General of Philadelphia, and the Reverend John Kelly of Albany, New York, accompanied by a young lay catechist, sailed for Africa late in 1841. They arrived and established themselves in the Maryland colony at Cape Palmas late in January, 1842. Monsignor Barron, having meanwhile been designated prefect apostolic of Upper Guinea, with responsibilities extending from Liberia to the Gold Coast, left soon to raise funds in the United States and later to seek additional missionaries in France. While in France, he was promoted to bishop, and his mission was raised to the status of a vicariate apostolic; but in spite of a promising beginning, when he arrived again in Africa he was greeted with news of disaster. Already two of the seven French priests whom he had sent ahead had died. The young lay catechist had also died, and Father Kelly, his health broken, had given up and returned to America. One by one, the remaining priests were succumbing to the fever, and in 1844 Bishop Barron petitioned to be discharged from his impossible responsibilities and allowed to return to the United States. The sole survivor among the priests from France, Father J.R. Bessieux, transferred himself to Gabon, hoping, like the Protestants of the American Board, to escape the high death rate. There he grimly remained, and his labors may be considered the beginning of Roman Catholic missions in that part of Africa.[131]

It is impossible in a brief discussion to relate all of the missionary efforts made by Americans or sponsored in the United States for the conversion of West Africa in the early part of the nineteenth century. The experiences of the missionaries of the American Board in Liberia and of the Baptists in Nigeria, however, are illustrative of the difficulties encountered, and the results achieved, by the devout,

---

[131] Ralph M. Wiltgen, Gold Coast Mission History, 1471-1880 (Techny, Ill., 1956), pp. 115-119; Du Plessis, The Evangelisation of Pagan Africa, p. 334.

hopeful, enthusiastic men and women who took it upon themselves to carry the message of Christianity to pagan Africa. Since the United States did not share in the later partition of Africa and the flag of the United States was never planted over an African empire, American missionaries have not received the historical credit which is their due. In many parts of Africa they were the first missionary pioneers.

West Africa was not the only part of the continent in which missionaries of the American Board labored to evangelize. Simultaneously with John Leighton Wilson's efforts in West Africa, a group of American missionaries was devoting itself to converting the natives of South Africa. In 1832 Dr. John Philip, superintendent of the London Missionary Society's missions in South Africa, received a letter from a young American Christian enthusiast named Purney, asking for information on missionary needs and conditions in the country. Purney, who was a student at Princeton Theological Seminary, was writing on behalf of a student organization of which he was an active member, the Society of Inquiry on the Subject of Missions to the Heathen.

Dr. Philip found Purney's letter awaiting him when he returned to Cape Town from a tour of several months covering the London Society's missions and stations on the frontiers of the colony. During his journey he had noted vast regions and whole tribes without a missionary--and it was beyond the resources of the London Missionary Society to provide people to labor in such places. Philip replied to Purney at once in a long, detailed, and informative letter, in which he strongly emphasized that there was a "noble field for missionary labour" among the "Zoolahs." He added that the two principal chiefs (or kings), Dingaan and Mosalekatsi, were friendly and highly favorable toward having missionaries among their people.[132]

---

[132] D.J. Kotzé (ed.), Letters of the American Missionaries, 1835-1838 (Cape Town, 1950), pp. 8-15; Missionary Herald, XXIX (1833), 414-420; Phillips, "Protestant America and the Pagan World," p. 212. The

All information which the student society received was forwarded to the American Board, which thus came into possession of Dr. Philip's letter. The letter was published in full in the November, 1833, issue of the Missionary Herald, and in the next issue the Board published the notice, "A mission [is]...contemplated to the Zoolahs, a populous tribe on the southeastern coast of Africa." A number of volunteers offered themselves, and in December, 1834, the first group of six missionaries, with their wives, sailed from Boston for South Africa. The group included Henry Isaac Venable, Daniel Lindley, Alexander Erwin Wilson, Aldin Grout, George Champion, and Newton Adams. Wilson and Adams, in addition to being ordained ministers, were also physicians and thus may be considered among the first medical missionaries.

The voyage to South Africa consumed several months; after arriving at Cape Town, the missionaries had to procure necessary equipment and supplies, begin the study of native languages, and complete their final preparations. Thus, more than a year elapsed between their departure from Boston and their arrival at the places where they hoped to establish their missions and implant Christianity. In the summer of 1836, Lindley, Wilson, and Venable finally reached Moseka, far beyond the Vaal River, the outer limit of civilization at the time. Adams, Grout, and Champion established themselves in Natal, near the coast and somewhat closer to civilization, but still on the far frontier.

The climate of South Africa is healthful and well suited to Europeans, but still the three who went beyond the Vaal suffered, and Mrs. Wilson died shortly after they reached Moseka. The remainder of the party recovered and for weeks labored with their own hands, erecting necessary buildings and making their surroundings habitable. They were completely isolated from civilization; everything depended entirely upon their own efforts.

---

names of the two Zulu chiefs are spelled in various ways by different authors. The present authors have chosen to follow the forms used by Dr. Philip in his letter to Purney.

They had barely completed their mission buildings when they found themselves in the midst of perils as likely to prove fatal, both to themselves and to their hopes, as the dreaded diseases of West Africa. Their mission was directly in the path of the restless Boers from the Cape who were beginning to migrate northward--the "Great Trek." In September, 1836, very shortly after the missionaries' arrival at Moseka, the local Matabele warriors attacked a party of emigrants, murdering some fifteen and stealing their sheep and cattle. A few weeks later Mosalekatsi attacked a second party, but was repulsed with the loss of a large number of his warriors. In the following January, 1837, a Boer commando (a fighting band of mounted burghers) retaliated, and the Americans found themselves, literally, in the thick of bitter fighting. At this time the Boers often regarded the Matabele somewhat as their contemporaries on the American frontier regarded Indians--as so much dangerous vermin, to be exterminated as quickly and ruthlessly as possible. Although the Americans almost miraculously escaped harm in the battle that took place around their mission, the mission house was riddled by bullets and assagais (short spears), and they decided to return to the coast under protection of the Boers. The danger was too great that the Africans might regard any white man as an enemy and fail to distinguish between friends and foes.

Wilson wrote to the Board on April 17, 1837:

> Early in the morning [January 17] I was awakened by the firing of guns; I arose and...saw the farmers on horseback, pursuing and shooting the natives, who were flying in every direction. As soon as they had finished the work of destruction at the village near us, the commander [probably Andries Hendrik Potgieter] rode to the house and assured us that they intended no harm against us or our property, and invited us to leave the country with them, as they thought it would not be safe for us to stay behind.... It now became a question with us, what was the path of duty.... There was some reason to fear that Moselekatsi and his people would no longer regard us as their friends. Even if there had been no reason to think thus, yet it was

> plain that our field of labor was destroyed....
>
> This emigration of the farmers from the colony, is going to form a new era in the history of the native tribes beyond the colony.... We are now on our way to join our brethren in the country of Dingaan. We have our fears, that the farmers and Dingaan will come into conflict in a few years.[133]

At the coast, Wilson, Venable, and Lindley joined the Americans who had remained in Natal, working among the coastal Zulus. Champion, Grout, and Adams appeared to be making progress. They had readily obtained the consent of Dingaan to their establishing a mission, and they had made a considerable number of converts and commenced the publication of textbooks and religious works in the Zulu language. But Dr. Wilson's fears as to Dingaan's future actions were well founded. Restless Boer farmers from the Cape were moving into Natal in large numbers. Dingaan became fearful for the freedom of his domain and his people and decided to end the danger, once and for all, by the complete extermination of the unwelcome immigrants. Early in June, 1837, Champion noted in his journal that the Zulus were preparing for war. In January, 1838, an immigrant party headed by Piet Retief, a noted Boer leader, entered Dingaan's domain and endeavored to negotiate for lands and permission to settle. The negotiations seemed to be proceeding smoothly, but Dingaan was merely biding his time. On February 6, he invited Retief to a conference at the royal kraal. Retief and his group entered unarmed, according to custom. At a signal from Dingaan, the entire Boer party, about sixty in number, was set upon and murdered. In the next few days, all over Natal, hundreds of Boer settlers died under the war clubs and assagais of the Zulu warriors.

Dingaan sent messengers to the missionaries, English and American, to assure them of his friendship and protection, but in the existing horrors they could not feel safe. His benevolence did not extend

---

[133] Missionary Herald, XXXIII (1837), 337-339, 416-421.

to their native converts; many of them were from other tribes for whom the Zulus felt the utmost contempt. They were slaughtered like cattle, and there was always the grim possibility that at some critical moment the king might not be able to control his maddened warriors. Consequently, the missionaries decided to leave the country. After a journey full of perils and hardships, they finally reached Port Natal, where they were able to take refuge on board a British ship. Lindley courageously agreed to remain behind for a time to keep in touch with the situation, but even he, at last, decided that it was preferable to be a live missionary than a pointlessly dead martyr.[134]

Dingaan's rising was, of course, crushed, and the massacre of Retief's party avenged, but while the battle was in progress it put an effective stop to all missionary effort in Natal. The Board decided to discontinue its missions, and the American missionaries were authorized to return to America. Lindley and Adams, however, elected to remain. Even before the outbreak of the war with Dingaan, Lindley had become friendly with the simple, hard-working Boer farmers who were migrating to Natal from the Cape in large numbers. They were without a minister, and upon finding that the theology of the Dutch Reformed Church was essentially the same as that of his own church, Lindley gladly accepted a call to be their pastor. For several years he ministered among them, traveling summer and winter, regardless of his own comfort or safety, to wherever his services might be needed. When the British authorities and the migrating Boers came to open blows in the early 1840's, he stuck to his post, ministering to the British prisoners of war as well as his Boers. He staunchly stood up for the rights of the conquered Zulus against his Boer parishioners. He so far gained the trust of everyone that in 1847, after the annexation of Natal by Great Britain, he was placed on the official payroll as a

---

[134] _Ibid._, XXXIV (1838), 307-314.

government missionary--an appointment that continued after the American Board resumed its South African efforts and Lindley re-entered its service.

Nor was the field of faith and worship the only one on which the handful of American missionaries left their impression. The Dutch farmers migrating into Natal found that some sort of government was necessary. With their highly democratic and independent-minded traditions, a republican government was inevitable. With a little disorder, but not much, a republic with an elected assembly (the *Volksraad*) was established. The government was weak at first and had to struggle to establish its authority.

> By the end of 1840 [the *Volksraad*] was finding its feet. Helped doubtless by the gift of a copy of the United States Constitution from one of the American missionaries, it had developed its procedure by trial and error, fixed a reasonable franchise, regularized candidature and election, done something to instil a sense of duty into its officials, and even checked the vagaries of public meetings and petitions.[135]

Dr. Newton Adams, like Lindley, gained the trust and affection of the people with whom he came into contact. In 1847 he was named as mediator on a commission to supervise the apportionment of land in Natal. But Adams, for reasons deep in his own mind and conscience, was unsympathetic toward the Zulus. So the governor, to redress the balance, named Lindley to the commission, "no doubt because of his known fairmindedness and also, possibly because he was *persona grata* with the Boers and familiar with their views."[136]

---

[135] Eric Anderson Walker, *The Great Trek* (London, 1938), p. 216.

[136] Sir George E. Cory, *The Rise of South Africa*, IV (London, 1926), 190; see also Edwin William Smith, *The Life and Times of Daniel Lindley (1801-1880), Missionary to the Zulus, Pastor of the Voortrekkers Ubebe Umhlope* (London, 1949), pp. 225, 250-251.

A major problem faced by both the short-lived Republic of Natal and the succeeding British colonial regime was that of coexistence with the Zulus while, at the same time, rendering them incapable of future mischief. The solution decided upon, largely as a result of the land commission's labors, was the establishment of a series of "locations," similar to the Indian reservations then being established in various parts of the United States. This solution seemed eminently fair and humane to people of the time and appealed especially to missionaries (including the Americans) because the Zulus, whose numbers were increasing daily by immigrants from across the Tugela River, could thereby be protected from the rapacity of settlers and traders, and would be available in numbers for teaching.[137] It is not unreasonable to suppose--although this is purely conjectural--that Adams and Lindley, who were members of the land commission and had some knowledge of the Indian problem in the United States, may have influenced the decision. It is possible, too, that Aldin Grout, who enjoyed considerable influence among the Boers, may have suggested locations to the people of Natal as a humane means of solving the problem.

Since the missionaries' major work lay among native peoples with whom they could not communicate without learning the native tongues, language study was an important part of their program. James C. Bryant and Lewis Grout, both of whom arrived in 1846, especially distinguished themselves as linguists and made lasting contributions to the study of South African linguistics. Bryant, who had a natural aptitude, picked up the local idiom so quickly that he was able to deliver a sermon in Zulu only ten weeks after his arrival. Eighteen months later he wrote an article on the Zulu language which is still considered

---

[137] Missionary Herald, XXXVI (1840), 247-248; XLIV (1848), 196-198.

one of the most concise and accurate accounts.[138]

Bryant unfortunately contracted tuberculosis, which was aggravated by exposure in all sorts of weather, and he died only two years after his arrival at the mission. During the last several months of his life, unable to preach or to perform the usual duties of a minister, he devoted himself to linguistic studies and to translating and writing. He found a capable and enthusiastic collaborator in Lewis Grout, who was destined to live a long and active life. "James [Bryant] taught him all that he knew and had the comforting realization that. . . Lewis Grout would continue with the translation of the Bible into Zulu and with the provision of lesson-helps and textbooks."[139]

To the early missionaries the world also owes most of its knowledge of the cultures of the places and regions in which they worked. They were not conscious or intentional anthropologists--they observed native customs, practices, and mores not so much for the sake of information as for evidences of the presence of evil which they proposed to attack and destroy. Their observations were accurate and close and in many instances afford the only knowledge the present day has of tribal life in Africa before the indigenous cultures were sharply modified by the onset of European civilization.

---

[138] Eleanor S. Reuling, First Saint to the Zulus (Boston, 1960). The Bryant article was published in the Journal of the American Oriental Society, I (1849), 385-396. It is interesting to note that the same volume includes linguistic articles by John Leighton Wilson and Lewis Grout.

[139] Reuling, First Saint to the Zulus, p. 38.

III. EXPLORERS AND FRONTIERSMEN

Other Americans leaving their mark upon Africa were neither seeking profits from trade nor concerned deeply with the salvation of souls, but loved adventure for its own sake. Among these must be included the score or more anonymous Americans numbered in the garrisons of Mozambique and the Portuguese captaincies in East Africa in the 1790's. They may have been fugitives from justice, or they may have been sailors or farm boys from New England impelled by romantic dreams, but there they were--Americans in the Portuguese army in Africa.[140]

One of the first to venture beyond the confines of America purely for the satisfaction of seeing something that no white man had ever seen before was John Ledyard, of Groton, Connecticut. Born in 1751, he received the usual New England grammar school education. For a time he studied law, but found it uninteresting. He next entered Dartmouth College, with a view to becoming a missionary among the Indians; but this dream soon palled, and he shipped before the mast on a voyage to Europe. At Gibraltar he jumped ship and enlisted in the British army, but the military authorities returned him to his ship. Following a brief visit home, he went to London in 1776 and offered himself to Captain James Cook, who was assembling a crew for his third voyage of exploration. Cook was evidently impressed favorably; the young Yankee was enlisted for the voyage as a corporal in the Royal Marines, and thus he discovered his life's inspiration and work. He was captivated by the unknown wilderness which Cook's ship touched, especially by the possibilities of what is now called the Pacific Northwest. A few years later he undertook a walking trip across Europe and through

---

[140] Mabel V. Jackson, European Powers and South-east Africa: A Study of International Relations on the South-east Coast of Africa, 1796-1856 (London, 1942), pp. 24-25.

Siberia to the Pacific. He traveled without permission of the Russian government, but he got as far as Irkutsk, in Siberia (and was undoubtedly the first American to penetrate into that part of Asia); there he was caught and summarily expelled from Russia, with a warning not to come back.

Ledyard had attracted the favorable attention of Sir Joseph Banks, the president of the Royal Society and one of the moving spirits in a new Association for Promoting the Discovery of the Interior Parts of Africa, which was founded in 1788. Upon arriving in London from his Siberian misadventure, he went immediately to Banks, who found him to be just the man needed in an effort to discover the source, course, and mouth of the Niger. Asked when he could start, he replied, "Tomorrow morning."

Ledyard did not get beyond Cairo--he contracted a fatal disease and died before he was fairly under way. Nevertheless, the information he transmitted before his death was considered invaluable, and his reports on Egypt were models of what the association wanted. Behind a façade of impulsiveness, he planned coolly and carefully, leaving nothing foreseeable to chance. His death, in January, 1789, was a great loss to African exploration.[141]

Another American who threw some light into the darkness that surrounded Africa was Archibald Robbins, even though he never penetrated into the regions south of the Sahara. Robbins, a native of Connecticut, after passing a considerable part of the War of 1812 as a prisoner of war, embarked in 1815 on the brig Commerce for a voyage to Gibraltar. The vessel was wrecked in September of that year near Cape Barbas, in what is now Río de Oro, and the survivors were captured and enslaved by the desert Arabs. Robbins spent three years

---

[141] "John Ledyard," by W.H. Ghent, in the Dictionary of American Biography, Vol. XI.

in slavery, accompanying his nomadic master over a wide area of northwestern Africa. He was a careful observer, and his narrative of his travels constitutes one of the earliest firsthand accounts of a region which is still little known.[142]

The mystery of the vast interior of Africa exerted a fascination upon the minds of many people. Even the scholarly Jared Sparks, clergyman, educator, chaplain of the United States Senate, and idolatrous biographer of George Washington, in his youth caught the fever. He visualized himself as an African explorer, crossing the great desert, going from "Tombucto" to the mouth of the Niger, "wherever it may be," and to other unknown parts of the continent.

Nothing ever came of Sparks's plan--it was a romantic dream--but it revealed both the ignorance of Africa among educated people and the extent to which Africa had excited the curiosity of Europe and America.[143] As the nineteenth century unfolded, the fog of ignorance and myth that blanketed the continent was gradually dispelled by explorers and adventurers of many nations. But this was not easily done. One of the major obstacles to investigation of the African interior was the determination of many of the coastal tribes that no European should pass through their territories. The Africans of the seacoast were middlemen between the white traders and the people of the interior; they effectively controlled the highly lucrative traffic in slaves, ivory, gold dust, and other products that came from deep in the continent. The coastal tribes feared that if Europeans succeeded in getting to the interior, their own position would be lost and their monopoly destroyed.

John Leighton Wilson and his fellow missionaries repeatedly

---

[142] Archibald Robbins, A Journal, Comprising an Account of the Loss of the Brig Commerce, of Hartford... (Hartford, Conn., 1836).

[143] George E. Ellis, "Memoir of Jared Sparks, LL.D.," Proceedings of the Massachusetts Historical Society, X (1867-1869), 226-227.

reported to the American Board that Africans had refused to let them pass, using every expedient to block the way from the coast. Paul du Chaillu, commencing his explorations, found that his boyhood friends at the mouth of the Gabon were determined to dissuade him from going inland.[144] It was not until Africans learned to fear the white man's weapons and power that the rivers and trails into the heart of the continent were open to the explorer.[145] This is not to say that the European and American punitive forces that landed from time to time at different places on the African coast came for the explicit purpose of making the country safe for explorers. Such expeditions had other and more immediate missions, but opening the gates to the interior was an accidental by-product of military punishment and conquest. And even though the United States never harbored any ambitions toward an African empire, American interests required punitive measures on several occasions, to prove to Africans that it was unwise to offer violence to Americans.

When Commodore Matthew C. Perry arrived on the West African Coast in 1842, with the first American squadron to be stationed permanently in African waters under the recent Webster-Ashburton Treaty with Great Britain, one of his first concerns was to look into cases of outrage and violence against American traders. The crew of an American vessel, the Mary Carver, has been massacred at Beribi, on the

---

[144] Explorations and Adventures in Equatorial Africa (New York, 1861), pp. 27, 226, 260, 478. Du Chaillu's career is sketched later. Tribes in the interior, too, frequently tried to keep a monopoly of trade with tribes beyond them. Thus, the Matabele of southern Africa made strong efforts to keep the Europeans from passing through Matabeleland.

[145] For additional examples of Africans' opposition to European commercial penetration of the interior see Kenneth Onwuka Dike, Trade and Politics in the Niger Delta, 1830-1885 (Oxford, 1956), pp. 206-207.

Ivory Coast. At a village called Fishtown, two men from the schooner Edward Burley had been killed, and Captain J.R. Brown, of the bark Atlanta, had been viciously attacked. The people of Fishtown were also boycotting all American traders and threatening to attack the nearby settlements of the Maryland Colonization Society at Cape Palmas.

Perry acted promptly. A landing force from his ships destroyed Beribi and killed the local king and several of his warriors in the fighting. At Fishtown, with his ships' guns trained threateningly on the town, Perry went ashore with such a display of pomp and power that there was no resistance. A brief investigation exonerated the tribesmen for killing two sailors from the Edward Burley; it was found that the Americans had started the trouble. But for boycotting Americans and threatening the American settlements, Perry exacted a penalty. He compelled the tribesmen to evacuate the town and move inland from the coast; he then burned the town.

Perry's measures were ruthless, but resulted in an end of the boycott, security for the Maryland settlements, and safety for white men on that part of the African coast for a long time to come.[146] Other nations and other navies also took sharp action on the African coast from time to time, until a white man was no longer stopped just beyond the high-tide mark by jealous Africans guarding their own monopolies.

American adventurers, explorers, and missionaries were among those foremost in taking advantage of the new possibilities, and among the most notable was Paul Belloni du Chaillu. As his name indicates, he was of French blood and birth--descendant of a long line of Huguenot ancestors. Because his father was connected with a French commercial house having extensive African interests, Du Chaillu spent several of

---

[146] Andrew H. Foote, Africa and the American Flag (New York, 1854), pp. 235-238.

the formative years of his youth in Africa, at a trading post on the Gabon River, of which his father was in charge. He migrated to the United States in the early 1850's, to Philadelphia, and became a naturalized citizen. Throughout his adult life and career he continued to regard himself as an American. Sponsored by the Philadelphia Academy of Science, he returned to Africa in 1855 for the express purpose of scientific exploration in an area which was still terra incognita to the world at large.

Du Chaillu based himself at the Gabon, where he had lived as a youth--"My arrival," he reported, "was hailed with joy by my former acquaintances, who thought I had come back to trade." Upon being assured that Du Chaillu did not intend to trade, his Mpongwe friends were puzzled and became alarmed lest he should "secretly try to wrest the trade of the interior out of their hands." Availing himself of the hospitality of the American missionaries at the Gabon, Du Chaillu acclimated himself and assembled the stores and equipment he would need.

With his boyhood knowledge of Africa reinforced by information he obtained from the missionaries, Du Chaillu spent several years systematically exploring and collecting specimens of the flora and fauna on both sides of the Gabon and deep into the unknown interior. When his reports were published, the detail that made him both famous and controversial was his assertion that somewhere in the tropical forest was a species of giant apes--gorillas. He had collected an impressive amount of evidence, but had been unable to obtain a specimen.

Du Chaillu was greeted with disbelief, almost with hoots and jeers, by savants who had never been in Africa. Many naturalists and biologists asserted vehemently that no such creatures existed outside Du Chaillu's imagination, despite the fact that John Leighton Wilson had forwarded convincing evidence previously and several skeletons and pelts had been sent to Europe by others. As for Du Chaillu's geographical observations, the famous German explorer Heinrich Barth, who had not been in the part of Africa Du Chaillu traversed, gravely asserted that Du Chaillu's map was the product of a mind deranged by fever; mountains could not possibly exist, nor rivers flow, where they were shown.[147]

A second expedition into Africa was led by Du Chaillu in 1863, and this time he brought back evidence of the gorilla that could not be controverted. This was fortunate, for on the second trip he made a discovery even more startling and unbelievable than that of the giant apes: deep in the tropical forest dwelt a race of pygmies--tiny human beings whose very existence was previously unsuspected by the civilized world.[148] Although there were references to the pygmies in a number of ancient Egyptian documents, such people were thought to be purely mythical. By the time Du Chaillu announced his discovery, however, the world had become accustomed to the idea that Africa hid unbelievable marvels. His veracity was no longer questioned.

The discoveries of the gorilla and the pygmies were enough, in themselves, to place Du Chaillu in the forefront of scientists and explorers. Unfortunately for his later fame, he was soon to be overshadowed by the more spectacular and more widely publicized achievements of another explorer, Henry M. Stanley. But it was Du Chaillu who had pioneered in the opening of Africa.

The Civil War in the United States marks a dividing line in many phases of American life, and nowhere is the division more conspicuous and significant than in American relations with Africa. By the destruction

---

[147]Du Chaillu, Explorations and Adventures in Equatorial Africa, passim. See articles on Du Chaillu by Alfred H. Guernsey in Harper's Magazine, XXXVI (1867-1868), 582-594; XXXVIII (1868-1869), 164-174; and XL (1869-1870), 201-213. See also Michel Vaucaire, Paul du Chaillu: Gorilla Hunter (New York, 1930), pp. 1-11.

[148]Du Chaillu, The Country of the Dwarfs (New York, 1872).

of the major stronghold of slavery in the Western world, the war brought about the virtual end of American participation in the slave trade. With emancipation and with the opening of a greater degree of opportunity for Negroes than they had ever had before in the United States, schemes for migration and colonization died a natural death. For a wide variety of reasons, direct American trade with Africa declined almost to the vanishing point; the American merchant marine to all intents and purposes disappeared from the seas. The American nation turned its attention increasingly to the vast, undeveloped regions of its own continent, leaving Africa to Europeans. Africa was carved up and divided among the powers of Europe; the American flag was never officially hoisted over a single port or stretch of beach.

Nevertheless, during the first half of the nineteenth century, the impact of the United States upon Africa as a whole was probably as decisive in its ultimate effects as that of any other country. Vast regions of Africa became aware of the products of the West because of the commercial activities of American traders. American missionaries were among the pioneers in the effort to bring Christianity to the natives. Adventurously inclined American explorers and scientists were among the first in investigating the mysteries of the African interior. Further, it cannot be doubted that fear of possible American encroachment in Africa and jealousy of the success of the American trader in commerce with the African natives contributed momentum to the annexation of African territories by imperialistic European powers.

American interest in Africa did not end after the Civil War, however. Missionaries continued with their work, and there were Americans who were fascinated by the lure of the unknown or by the promise of opportunities denied them in North America. American interest in Africa in the latter part of the nineteenth century was quiescent rather than dead. It was merely waiting to be aroused by the exploits of Stanley and by the discovery of gold, copper, diamonds, and of products unknown to the shipmasters and traders of an earlier age.

BIBLIOGRAPHY

I. Unpublished Materials and Microfilms

Bowen, Thomas Jefferson. THE THOMAS JEFFERSON BOWEN PAPERS. MSS held by the Southern Baptist Convention Historical Commission, Nashville, Tenn. The Hoover Institution has a copy of them on microfilm; 1 reel.

Brooks, George E. "AMERICAN LEGITIMATE TRADE WITH WEST AFRICA, 1789-1914." Unpublished Ph.D. dissertation, Boston University, 1962. 281 pp.

Harr, Wilber Christian. "THE NEGRO AS AN AMERICAN PROTESTANT MISSIONARY IN AFRICA." Unpublished Ph.D. dissertation, University of Chicago Divinity School, 1945. 214 pp.

Howard, Lawrence Cabot. "AMERICAN INVOLVEMENT IN AFRICA SOUTH OF THE SAHARA, 1800-1860." Unpublished Ph.D. dissertation, Harvard University, 1956. 347 pp.

Phillips, Clifton Jackson. "PROTESTANT AMERICA AND THE PAGAN WORLD: THE FIRST HALF CENTURY OF THE AMERICAN BOARD OF COMMISSIONERS FOR FOREIGN MISSIONS." Unpublished Ph.D. dissertation, Harvard University, 1954. 359 pp.

II. Published Materials

A. Articles

Alagoa, E.J. "PRELIMINARY INVENTORY OF THE RECORDS OF THE UNITED STATES DIPLOMATIC AND CONSULAR POSTS IN WEST AFRICA, 1856-1913," Journal of the Historical Society of Nigeria, Vol. II, No. 1 (December, 1960).

Albion, Robert Greenhalgh. "FROM SAILS TO SPINDLES: ESSEX COUNTY IN TRANSITION," Essex Institute Historical Collections, XCV (1959), 115-136.

Bennett, Norman Robert. "AMERICANS IN ZANZIBAR, 1825-1845," Essex Institute Historical Collections, XCV (1959), 239-262.

_______. "WILLIAM H. HATHORNE, MERCHANT AND CONSUL IN ZANZIBAR," Essex Institute Historical Collections, XCIX (1963), 117-146.

Bratter, Herbert M. "JONATHAN LAMBERT OF SALEM, THE YANKEE WHO WOULD BE KING," Essex Institute Historical Collections, LXXXVIII (1952), 150-162.

Brent, John Carroll. "LEAVES FROM AN AFRICAN JOURNAL," Knickerbocker Magazine, XXXIII (1849), 41-48, 116-127, 206-215, 334-340, 399-409; XXXIV (1850), 127-133, 227-234, 300-305.

Carneiro, Don Jacinto Pereira. "MEMOIR ON THE TRADE TO THE WEST COAST OF AFRICA NORTHWARD OF THE EQUATOR," The Nautical Magazine and Naval Chronicle for 1855, pp. 407-415.

Eilts, Hermann Frederick. "AHMAD BIN NA'AMAN'S MISSION TO THE UNITED STATES IN 1840: THE VOYAGE OF AL-SULTANAH TO NEW YORK CITY," Essex Institute Historical Collections, XCVIII (1962), 219-277.

"EXTRACT OF CAPT. E. PREBLE'S JOURNAL ON BOARD THE ESSEX," Essex Institute Historical Collections, X, Part III (1869), 60-108.

Fisher, Miles Mark. "LOTT CARY, THE COLONIZING MISSIONARY," Journal of Negro History, VII (1922), 380-418.

Furber, Holden. "THE BEGINNINGS OF AMERICAN TRADE WITH INDIA, 1784-1812," New England Quarterly, XI (1938), 235-265.

Fyfe, Christopher. "THE COUNTESS OF HUNTINGDON'S CONNEXION IN NINETEENTH CENTURY SIERRA LEONE," Sierra Leone Bulletin of Religion, IV, No. 2 (1962), 53-61.

_______. "THE WEST AFRICAN METHODISTS IN THE NINETEENTH CENTURY," Sierra Leone Bulletin of Religion, III, No. 1 (1961), 22-28.

Ghent, W.H. "JOHN LEDYARD," Dictionary of American Biography, Vol. XI.

Guernsey, Alfred H. "DU CHAILLU, GORILLAS AND CANNIBALS," Harper's Magazine, XXXVI (1867-1868), 582-594.

_______. "PAUL DU CHAILLU AGAIN," Harper's Magazine, XXXVIII (1868-1869), 164-174.

_______. "PAUL DU CHAILLU ONCE MORE," Harper's Magazine, XL (1869-1870), 201-213.

Hewes, Edwin B. "JONATHAN LAMBERT OF SALEM, KING OF TRISTAN D'ACUNHA," Essex Institute Historical Collections, LXXI (1935), 1-6.

_______. "NATHANIEL BOWDITCH, SUPERCARGO AND MARINER," Essex Institute Historical Collections, LXX (1934), 209-226.

Johnston, William D. "SLAVERY IN RHODE ISLAND, 1755-1776," Publications of the Rhode Island Historical Society, II (1894), 113-164.

Kirk-Greene, A.H.M. "AMERICA IN THE NIGER VALLEY: A COLONIZATION CENTENARY," Phylon, XXIII (1962), 225-239.

"LETTERS FROM DAVID LIVINGSTONE, THE DISTINGUISHED AFRICAN EXPLORER, WRITTEN IN 1856," Essex Institute Historical Collections, XII (1874), 285-294.

McKey, Richard H., Jr. "ELIAS HASKET DERBY AND THE FOUNDING OF THE EASTERN TRADE," Essex Institute Historical Collections, XCVIII (1962), 1-25, 65-83.

Mehlinger, Louis R. "THE ATTITUDE OF THE FREE NEGRO TOWARD AFRICAN COLONIZATION," Journal of Negro History, I (1916), 276-301.

Miller, Thomas. "WESTERN AFRICA: ITS COAST, RESOURCES, AND TRADE," The Nautical Magazine and Naval Chronicle for 1855, pp. 291-296, 345-355.

THE MISSIONARY HERALD (Boston), Vols. XXVIII-XCI, 1831-1895. Numerous references.

Rochon, Abbé. "A VOYAGE TO MADAGASCAR AND THE EAST INDIES," in John Pinkerton (ed.), A General Collection of the Best and Most Interesting Voyages and Travels in All Parts of the World (London, 1808-1814), Vol. XVI.

Routh, E.C. "THOMAS JEFFERSON BOWEN," in The Encyclopedia of Southern Baptists (Nashville, 1958).

Seaver, Benjamin. "MR. SEAVER'S LETTER CONCERNING THE ISLANDS OF TRISTAN D'ACUNHA," Historical Collections of the Massachusetts Historical Society, Ser. 2, II (1814), 125-128.

Sherwood, Henry Noble. "Paul Cuffe," Journal of Negro History, VIII, No. 2 (1923), 153-229.

Toussaint, A. "EARLY AMERICAN TRADE WITH MAURITIUS," Essex Institute Historical Collections, LXXXVII (1951), 373-387.

Tucker, Jonathan. "THE FIRST VOYAGE TO INDIA FROM SALEM, 1786-1787," Essex Institute Historical Collections, LXXV (1939), 44-52.

B. Source Material--Autobiographies, Journals, Personal Reminiscences, etc.

AFRICA REDEEMED; OR, THE MEANS OF HER RELIEF: ILLUSTRATED BY THE GROWTH AND PROSPECTS OF LIBERIA. London, James Nisbet, 1851. 300 pp.

Alexander, Archibald. A HISTORY OF COLONIZATION ON THE WESTERN COAST OF AFRICA. Philadelphia, W.S. Martien, 1846. 603 pp.

Arnett, Benjamin William. BISHOP ABRAHAM GRANT'S TRIP TO THE WEST COAST OF AFRICA; REPORTED TO THE BISHOP'S COUNCIL AT TAWAWA CHIMNEY CORNER, WILBERFORCE, OHIO, JUNE 16, 1899. New York, published by Order of the Bishop's Council by Rev. H. B. Parks, 1899. 50 pp.

Ashmun, Jehudi. HISTORY OF THE AMERICAN COLONY IN LIBERIA, FROM DECEMBER 1821 TO 1823; COMPILED FROM THE AUTHENTIC RECORDS OF THE COLONY. Washington, Way and Gideon, 1826. 42 pp.

Bacon, Ephraim. ABSTRACT OF A JOURNAL KEPT BY E. BACON, UNITED STATES ASSISTANT AGENT FOR THE RECEPTION OF RECAPTURED NEGROES ON THE WESTERN COAST OF AFRICA: CONTAINING AN ACCOUNT OF THE FIRST NEGOTIATIONS FOR THE PURCHASE OF LANDS FOR THE AMERICAN COLONY. 4th ed. Philadelphia, Clark and Raser, 1824. 48 pp.

Bowdich, Thomas Edward. EXCURSIONS IN MADEIRA AND PORTO SANTO, DURING THE AUTUMN OF 1823, WHILE ON HIS THIRD VOYAGE TO AFRICA. London, G.B. Whittaker, 1825. 278 pp.

Bowen, Thomas Jefferson. CENTRAL AFRICA: ADVENTURES AND MISSIONARY LABORS IN SEVERAL COUNTRIES IN THE INTERIOR OF AFRICA, FROM 1849 TO 1856. Charleston, Southern Baptist Publication Society, 1857. 359 pp.

_______. GRAMMAR AND DICTIONARY OF THE YORUBA LANGUAGE, WITH AN INTRODUCTORY DESCRIPTION OF THE COUNTRY AND PEOPLE OF YORUBA. Washington, Smithsonian Institution, 1858. 136 pp.

_______. MEROKE; OR, MISSIONARY LIFE IN AFRICA. Revised by Rev. T.J. Bowen. Philadelphia, c1858. 207 pp.

Bridge, Horatio. JOURNAL OF AN AFRICAN CRUISER: COMPRISING SKETCHES OF THE CANARIES, THE CAPE DE VERDS, LIBERIA, MADEIRA, SIERRA LEONE, AND OTHER PLACES OF INTEREST ON THE WEST COAST OF AFRICA. Ed. by Nathaniel Hawthorne. New York, G.P. Putnam, 1853. 179 pp.

Brown, George S. BROWN'S ABRIDGED JOURNAL: CONTAINING A BRIEF ACCOUNT OF THE LIFE, TRIALS, AND TRAVELS OF GEORGE S. BROWN, SIX YEARS A MISSIONARY IN LIBERIA, WEST AFRICA. Troy, N.Y., Prescott and Wilson, 1849. 389 pp.

Campbell, Robert. A FEW FACTS RELATING TO LAGOS, ABEOKUTA, AND OTHER SECTIONS OF CENTRAL AFRICA. Philadelphia, King and Baird, 1860. 18 pp.

_______. A PILGRIMAGE TO MY MOTHERLAND: AN ACCOUNT OF A JOURNEY AMONG THE EGBAS AND YORUBAS OF CENTRAL AFRICA, IN 1859-60. New York, T. Hamilton, 1861. 145 pp.

Carnes, Joshua A. JOURNAL OF A VOYAGE FROM BOSTON TO THE WEST COAST OF AFRICA, WITH A FULL DESCRIPTION OF THE MANNER OF TRADING WITH THE NATIVES ON THE COAST. Boston, J.P. Jewett, 1852. 479 pp.

Christy, David. ETHIOPIA: HER GLOOM AND GLORY, AS ILLUSTRATED IN THE HISTORY OF THE SLAVE TRADE AND SLAVERY, THE RISE OF THE REPUBLIC OF LIBERIA, AND THE PROGRESS OF AFRICAN MISSIONS. Cincinnati, Rickey, Mallory and Webb, 1857. 255 pp.

Cleveland, H.W.S. VOYAGES OF A MERCHANT NAVIGATOR OF THE DAYS THAT ARE PAST; COMPILED FROM THE JOURNALS AND LETTERS OF THE LATE RICHARD J. CLEVELAND. New York, Harper, 1886. 245 pp.

Coker, Daniel. JOURNAL OF DANIEL COKER, A DESCENDANT OF AFRICA, FROM THE TIME OF LEAVING NEW YORK, IN THE SHIP ELIZABETH, CAPT. SEBOR, ON A VOYAGE FOR SHERBRO, IN AFRICA, IN COMPANY WITH THREE AGENTS, AND ABOUT NINETY PERSONS OF COLOUR. Baltimore, published by Edward J. Coale, in aid of the Funds of the Maryland Auxiliary Colonization Society, 1820; John D. Toy, printer. 52 pp.

Cox, Melville Beveridge. REMAINS OF MELVILLE B. COX, LATE MISSIONARY TO LIBERIA, WITH A MEMOIR. Boston, Light and Horton, 1835. 240 pp.

Delany, M.R. OFFICIAL REPORT OF THE NIGER VALLEY EXPLORING PARTY. New York, T. Hamilton, 1861. 75 pp.

Du Chaillu, Paul Belloni. ADVENTURES IN THE GREAT FOREST OF EQUATORIAL AFRICA AND THE COUNTRY OF THE DWARFS. New York, Harper, 1890. 476 pp.

_______. THE COUNTRY OF THE DWARFS. New York, Harper, 1872. 314 pp.

_______. EXPLORATIONS AND ADVENTURES IN EQUATORIAL AFRICA, WITH ACCOUNTS OF THE MANNERS AND CUSTOMS OF THE PEOPLE, AND OF THE CHASE OF THE GORILLA, THE CROCODILE, LEOPARD, ELEPHANT, HIPPOPOTAMUS, AND OTHER ANIMALS. New York, Harper, 1861. 531 pp.

Foote, Andrew Hull. AFRICA AND THE AMERICAN FLAG. New York, D. Appleton, 1854. 300 pp.

Grout, Lewis. ZULULAND; OR, LIFE AMONG THE ZULU-KAFIRS OF NATAL AND ZULULAND, SOUTH AFRICA. Philadephia, Presbyterian Publication Comm., 1864. 351 pp.

Gurley, Ralph Randolph. LIFE OF JEHUDI ASHMUN, LATE COLONIAL AGENT IN LIBERIA; WITH AN APPENDIX, CONTAINING EXTRACTS FROM HIS JOURNAL AND OTHER WRITINGS; WITH A BRIEF SKETCH OF THE LIFE OF REV. LOTT CARY. Washington, J.C. Dunn, 1835. 396 pp.

Hawkins, Joseph. A HISTORY OF A VOYAGE TO THE COAST OF AFRICA AND TRAVELS INTO THE INTERIOR OF THAT COUNTRY. Philadelphia, S.C. Ustick, 1797. 179 pp.

Hening, Mrs. E.F. HISTORY OF THE AFRICAN MISSION OF THE PROTESTANT EPISCOPAL CHURCH IN THE UNITED STATES, WITH MEMOIRS OF DECEASED MISSIONARIES, AND NOTICES OF NATIVE CUSTOMS. New York, Stanford and Swords, 1850. 300 pp.

Isaacs, Nathaniel. TRAVELS AND ADVENTURES IN EASTERN AFRICA. 2 vols. Cape Town, The Van Riebeeck Society, 1936. (Original ed., London, 1836.)

Kotzé, D.J. (ed.). LETTERS OF THE AMERICAN MISSIONARIES, 1835-1838. Cape Town, The Van Riebeeck Society, 1950. 294 pp.

MEMOIRS AND TRAVELS OF MAURITIUS AUGUSTUS COUNT DE BENYOWSKI. Ed. and Introd. by Captain S. Pasfield Oliver. London, Kegan Paul, Trench, Trübner and Co., 1904. 636 pp.

Morrell, Benjamin. A NARRATIVE OF FOUR VOYAGES TO THE SOUTH SEA, NORTH AND SOUTH PACIFIC OCEAN, CHINESE SEA, ETHIOPIC AND SOUTHERN ATLANTIC OCEAN, INDIAN AND ANTARCTIC OCEAN, FROM THE YEAR 1822 TO 1831. New York, J. and J. Harper, 1832. 492 pp.

Reynolds, Jeremiah N. VOYAGE OF THE UNITED STATES FRIGATE POTOMAC, UNDER THE COMMAND OF JOHN DOWNES, DURING THE CIRCUMNAVIGATION OF THE GLOBE, IN THE YEARS 1831, 1832, 1833, AND 1834. New York, Harper, 1835. 560 pp.

Robbins, Archibald. A JOURNAL, COMPRISING AN ACCOUNT OF THE LOSS OF THE BRIG COMMERCE, OF HARTFORD (CON.), JAMES RILEY, MASTER, UPON THE WESTERN COAST OF AFRICA, AUGUST 28TH, 1815; ALSO OF THE SLAVERY AND SUFFERING OF THE AUTHOR AND THE REST OF THE CREW, UPON THE DESERT OF THE ZAHARA, IN THE YEARS 1815, 1816, 1817; WITH ACCOUNTS OF THE MANNERS, CUSTOMS, AND HABITS OF THE WANDERING ARABS; ALSO, A BRIEF HISTORICAL AND GEOGRAPHICAL VIEW OF THE CONTINENT OF AFRICA. Hartford, S. Andrus, 1836. 275 pp.

Ruschenberger, William Samuel Waithman. A VOYAGE ROUND THE WORLD, INCLUDING AN EMBASSY TO MUSCAT AND SIAM IN 1835, 1836, AND 1837. Philadelphia, Carey, Lea and Blanchard, 1838. 559 pp.

Scott, Mrs. Anna M. (Steele). DAY DAWN IN AFRICA; OR, PROGRESS OF THE PROTESTANT EPISCOPAL MISSION AT CAPE PALMAS, WEST AFRICA. New York, Protestant Episcopal Society for the Promotion of Evangelical Knowledge, 1858. 314 pp.

Thomas, Charles W. ADVENTURES AND OBSERVATIONS ON THE WEST COAST OF AFRICA AND ITS ISLANDS: HISTORICAL AND DESCRIPTIVE SKETCHES OF MADEIRA, CANARY, BIAFRA AND CAPE VERDE ISLANDS; THEIR CLIMATE, INHABITANTS, AND PRODUCTIONS; ACCOUNTS OF PLACES, PEOPLES, CUSTOMS, TRADE, MISSIONARY OPERATIONS, ETC., ETC., ON THAT PART OF THE AFRICAN COAST LYING BETWEEN TANGIER, MOROCCO, AND BENGUELA. New York, Derby and Jackson, 1860. 479 pp.

C. Secondary Material

Albion, Robert Greenhalgh, and Pope, Jennie Barnes. SEA LANES IN WARTIME: THE AMERICAN EXPERIENCE, 1775-1942. London, George Allen and Unwin, 1943. 367 pp.

Anderson, Robert Earle. LIBERIA, AMERICA'S AFRICAN FRIEND. Chapel Hill, University of North Carolina Press, 1952. 305 pp.

APPLETON'S CYCLOPEDIA OF AMERICAN BIOGRAPHY. Eds. James Grant Wilson and John Fiske. 6 vols. New York, D. Appleton, 1888-1889.

Barclay, Wade Crawford. EARLY AMERICAN METHODISM, 1769-1844. 2 vols. New York, The Board of Missions and Church Extension of the Methodist Church, 1949-1950. (These two volumes together form Part I of the four-volume series, HISTORY OF METHODIST MISSIONS.)

Biddulph, John. THE PIRATES OF MALABAR AND AN ENGLISH-WOMAN IN INDIA TWO HUNDRED YEARS AGO. London, Smith, Elder, 1907. 327 pp.

Biobaku, Saburi O. THE EGBA AND THEIR NEIGHBOURS, 1842-1872. Oxford, Clarendon Press, 1957. 128 pp.

Brady, Cyrus Townsend. COMMERCE AND CONQUEST IN EAST AFRICA, WITH PARTICULAR REFERENCE TO THE SALEM TRADE WITH ZANZIBAR. Salem, Essex Institute, 1950. 245 pp.

Brawley, Benjamin Griffith. NEGRO BUILDERS AND HEROES. Chapel Hill, University of North Carolina Press, 1937. 315 pp.

Butt-Thompson, Frederick William. SIERRA LEONE IN HISTORY AND TRADITION. London, H.F. and G. Witherby, 1926. 275 pp.

Cartwright, Charles E. THE TALE OF OUR MERCHANT SHIPS. New York, E.P. Dutton, 1924. 275 pp.

Clauder, Anna Cornelia. AMERICAN COMMERCE AS AFFECTED BY THE WARS OF THE FRENCH REVOLUTION AND NAPOLEON, 1793-1812. Philadelphia, University of Pennsylvania, 1932. 264 pp.

Cory, Sir George Edward. THE RISE OF SOUTH AFRICA: A HISTORY OF THE ORIGIN OF SOUTH AFRICAN COLONISATION AND OF ITS DEVELOPMENT TOWARDS THE EAST FROM THE EARLIEST TIMES TO 1857. 5 vols. London, Longmans, Green, 1919-1930.

Coupland, Reginald. WILBERFORCE. 2d ed. London, Collins, 1945. 447 pp.

Cox-George, Noah Arthur William. FINANCE AND DEVELOPMENT IN WEST AFRICA: THE SIERRA LEONE EXPERIENCE. London, D. Dobson, 1961. 333 pp.

Crowder, Michael. THE STORY OF NIGERIA. London, Faber and Faber, 1962. 307 pp.

Curtin, Philip D. THE IMAGE OF AFRICA: BRITISH IDEAS AND ACTION, 1780-1850. Madison, University of Wisconsin Press, 1964. 526 pp.

Duignan, Peter, and Clendenen, Clarence. THE UNITED STATES AND THE AFRICAN SLAVE TRADE, 1619-1862. Stanford, Calif., Hoover Institution, 1963. 72 pp.

Dulles, Foster Rhea. THE OLD CHINA TRADE. Boston, Houghton Mifflin, 1930. 228 pp.

Du Plessis, Johannes. THE EVANGELISATION OF PAGAN AFRICA: A HISTORY OF CHRISTIAN MISSIONS TO THE PAGAN TRIBES OF CENTRAL AFRICA. Cape Town, J.C. Juta, 1930. 408 pp.

Fox, Early Lee. THE AMERICAN COLONIZATION SOCIETY, 1817-1840. Baltimore, The Johns Hopkins Press, 1919. 231 pp.

Freeman, Edward Augustus. THE EPOCH OF NEGRO BAPTISTS AND THE FOREIGN MISSION BOARD. Kansas City, Kans., Central Seminary Press, 1953. 301 pp.

Fyfe, Christopher. A HISTORY OF SIERRA LEONE. London, Oxford University Press, 1962. 773 pp.

Gammell, William. A HISTORY OF AMERICAN BAPTIST MISSIONS IN ASIA, AFRICA, EUROPE, AND NORTH AMERICA, UNDER THE CARE OF THE AMERICAN BAPTIST MISSIONARY UNION. Boston, Gould, Kendall and Lincoln, 1854. 359 pp.

Greenbie, Sydney, and Greenbie, Marjorie. GOLD OF OPHIR; OR, THE LURE THAT MADE AMERICA. Garden City, N.Y., Doubleday, Page, 1925. 330 pp.

Groves, Charles Pelham. THE PLANTING OF CHRISTIANITY IN AFRICA. 4 vols. London, Lutterworth Press, 1948-1958.

Hedges, James B. THE BROWNS OF PROVIDENCE PLANTATIONS: COLONIAL YEARS. Cambridge, Mass., Harvard University Press, 1952. 379 pp.

Henries, A. Doris Banks. THE LIBERIAN NATION: A SHORT HISTORY. New York, H. Jaffe, 1954. 250 pp.

Hodgkin, Thomas Lionel. NIGERIAN PERSPECTIVES: AN HISTORICAL ANTHROLOGY. London, Oxford University Press, 1960. 340 pp.

Hohman, Elmo Paul. THE AMERICAN WHALEMAN: A STUDY OF LIFE AND LABOR IN THE WHALING INDUSTRY. New York, Longmans, Green, 1928. 355 pp.

Howard, Warren S. AMERICAN SLAVERS AND THE FEDERAL LAW, 1837-1862. Berkeley, University of California Press, 1963. 336 pp.

Ingham, Ernest Graham. SIERRA LEONE AFTER A HUNDRED YEARS. London, Seeley, 1894. 368 pp.

Ingham, Kenneth. A HISTORY OF EAST AFRICA. London, Longmans, Green, 1962. 456 pp.

Isaacs, Harold Robert. THE NEW WORLD OF NEGRO AMERICANS. New York, John Day, 1963. 366 pp.

Jackson, Mabel V. EUROPEAN POWERS AND SOUTH-EAST AFRICA: A STUDY OF INTERNATIONAL RELATIONS ON THE SOUTH-EAST COAST OF AFRICA, 1796-1856. London, Longmans, Green, 1942. 284 pp.

Mackeurtan, Harold Graham. THE CRADLE DAYS OF NATAL (1497-1845). London, Longmans, Green, 1930. 348 pp.

Maclay, Edgar Stanton. A HISTORY OF THE UNITED STATES NAVY FROM 1775 TO 1893. 2 vols. New York, D. Appleton, 1894-1895.

Mannix, Daniel Pratt. BLACK CARGOES: A HISTORY OF THE ATLANTIC SLAVE TRADE, 1518-1865. In collaboration with Malcolm Cowley. New York, Viking Press, 1962. 306 pp.

Massachusetts Historical Society. THE COMMERCE OF RHODE ISLAND, 1726-1800. 2 vols. Boston, The Society, 1914-1915.

Metcalfe, G.E. MACLEAN OF THE GOLD COAST: THE LIFE AND TIMES OF GEORGE MACLEAN, 1801-1847. London, Oxford University Press, 1962. 344 pp.

Milburn, William. ORIENTAL COMMERCE: CONTAINING A GEOGRAPHICAL DESCRIPTION OF THE PRINCIPAL PLACES IN THE EAST INDIES, CHINA, AND JAPAN, WITH THEIR PRODUCE, MANUFACTURES, AND TRADE. 2 vols. London, Black, Parry, 1813.

Moore, Ernst D. IVORY, SCOURGE OF AFRICA. New York, Harper, 1931. 256 pp.

Morison, Samuel Eliot. THE MARITIME HISTORY OF MASSACHUSETTS, 1783-1860. Boston, Houghton Mifflin, 1921. 400 pp.

Phillips, James Duncan. SALEM AND THE INDIES: THE STORY OF THE GREAT COMMERCIAL ERA OF THE CITY. Boston, Houghton Mifflin, 1947. 468 pp.

Reuling, Eleanor S. FIRST SAINT TO THE ZULUS. Boston, American Board of Commissioners for Foreign Missions, 1960. 44 pp.

Rollin, Frank A. LIFE AND PUBLIC SERVICES OF MARTIN R. DELANY. Boston, Lee and Shepard, 1868. 367 pp.

Rosenthal, Eric. STARS AND STRIPES IN AFRICA: BEING A HISTORY OF AMERICAN ACHIEVEMENTS IN AFRICA BY EXPLORERS, MISSIONARIES, PIRATES, ADVENTURERS, HUNTERS, MINERS, MERCHANTS, SCIENTISTS, SOLDIERS, SHOWMEN, ENGINEERS AND OTHERS, WITH SOME ACCOUNT OF AFRICANS WHO HAVE PLAYED A PART IN AMERICAN AFFAIRS. London, G. Routledge, 1938. 306 pp.

Ross, Emory. OUT OF AFRICA. New York, Friendship Press, 1936. 216 pp.

Shaw, George A. MADAGASCAR AND FRANCE, WITH SOME ACCOUNT OF THE ISLAND, ITS PEOPLE, ITS RESOURCES AND DEVELOPMENT. London, The Religious Tract Society, 1885. 320 pp.

Smith, Edwin William. THE LIFE AND TIMES OF DANIEL LINDLEY (1801-1880), MISSIONARY TO THE ZULUS, PASTOR OF THE VOORTREKKERS UBEBE UMHLOPE. London, Epworth Press, 1949. 456 pp.

Southorn, Bella Sidney, Lady. THE GAMBIA: THE STORY OF THE GROUNDNUT COLONY. London, Allen and Unwin, 1952. 283 pp.

Spears, John Randolph. THE AMERICAN SLAVE-TRADE: AN ACCOUNT OF ITS ORIGIN, GROWTH AND SUPPRESSION. New York, Chas. Scribner's Sons, 1900. 232 pp.

Starbuck, Alexander. HISTORY OF THE AMERICAN WHALE FISHERY. Waltham, Mass., published by the author, 1878. 768 pp.

Staudenraus, P.J. THE AFRICAN COLONIZATION MOVEMENT, 1816-1865. New York, Columbia University Press, 1961. 323 pp.

Thompson, Mack. MOSES BROWN, RELUCTANT REFORMER. Chapel Hill, University of North Carolina Press, 1962. 316 pp.

Vaucaire, Michel. PAUL DU CHAILLU: GORILLA HUNTER. New York, Harper, 1930. 322 pp.

Walker, Eric Anderson. THE GREAT TREK. London, A. and C. Black, 1938. 388 pp.

White, Philip L. THE BEEKMANS OF NEW YORK IN POLITICS AND COMMERCE, 1647-1877. New York, New York Historical Society, 1956. 705 pp.

Wiltgen, Ralph M. GOLD COAST MISSION HISTORY, 1471-1880. Techny, Ill., Divine Word Publications, 1956. 181 pp.